Throughout My Passing Day

Throughout My Passing Day

Poems by
Harold G. Ross

Sunflower University Press ®
1531 Yuma (Box 1009), Manhattan, Kansas 66502-4228

© 1993 by Harold G. Ross

Printed in the United States of America on acid-free paper.

ISBN 0-89745-170-8

Layout by Lori L. Daniel

*Oh God,
how long I make you wait
before I see*

                        Dr. George S. Bascom
                        Repentance

I dedicate this to God; my children, David, Richard, Marcia, and Susan; my parents, Bert and Pearl Ross; my brothers, Earl, Art, Jim, and Don; and other relatives and friends; with a special thanks to my close friends George and Jane Bascom — George for his help and inspiration, Jane for her steadfast encouragement. To Bill and Joanne Michel, my mentor Ralph Mitchell, and to all those who have touched my life and made it better.

Contents

Life

That Ol' Bridge	1
Kansas Dust	2
Bicycle Ride	3
Suburb Morning	4
Country Morning	4
Las Vegas	5
When Nature Calls to Me	6
Ghetto Morning	6
The Open-Faced Spinner	7
A Brother	8
The Old House	9
She Wore a Rose	10
She Wore a Frown	11
The Rifle Shot	12
Nineteen Ninety	13
The Drowning	14
San Diego	15
When the Movie's Over	16
Fishing Man	17
My Children	19
The Old Meyers Place	21
Night Fishing	22
Mother's Funeral	23
Wanderlust	25
The Old Note	26
A Day for Fishing	27
The Quester	27
The Old Man and the Mirror	28
Father's Death (March 1963)	29
Mother's Death (August 1979)	31
He Smiled at Me	32

The Old Woman	33
Frontier Spirit	35
To the Sea	35
Boyhood Summer	37
Yesterdays	37
Nightfall on the Farm	38
Pooch	39
A Mother and Son	40
The Flood	41
Gone	42
Sunset Run	43
My Father's Death	44
Then Where	44
The Old Woman and the Nursing Home	45
The Roller Skater	46
Time's Grip	47
The Written Word	48
Just for Her Sake	49
The Tyrant	50
An Old Vacant House	51
The Train	52
Back to You	53
Clarks Creek	55
With Him Went Her Will to Trust	56
The Funeral	57
She Had No Secrets	58
A Pretty Lady	59
San Diego Bay	61
I Might Demure	61
The Old Mill	62
The Skull	63
A Loving Thought	64
The Wife	64
I Want to Go	65
Evening Brings All Things Home	67
A Day Splitting Wood	68
Life's Struggles	69
The Merry-Go-Round	70
Tough Cowboy	71
The Good Old Days	72
Robert E. Lee	73
A Pony for Kristin	75

Nature Will Decide	76
Winter Stagecoach Run	77
Farm Nostalgia	79
The Farmhouse	80
Good Days and Nights	80
Saturday Morning	81
My Brew Is Life	83
An Earth Full of Hope	84
Up to the Pasture	85
Winter Morning	87
A Dying Track	88
The Little Girl	89
Early Fishing	90
An Old Stone House	91
Some Spice	92
Silence	93
Depressed	93
A Friend Is Gone	94
Waited	95
Scientific Report	96
Early Morning Frontier Town	97
A Miniskirt (Early 1960s)	98
Dawn at the Bay	99
My Mother	99
Kansas City V.A. Hospital	100
Going Nowhere at All	101
Excluded	102

Nature

Twin Sycamores	105
The Undecided Leaf	106
Tumbleweeds	106
Dark Before the Dawn	107
The Cricket	107
Tuttle Sunset	108
Morning Clouds	109
A Shady Nook	111
Hot Summer Day	111
Along the Broken Hills	112
The Windowpane	112
Summer Raindrops	113

Sunset	113
Bluestem Grass	114
An Old-Time August	115
Sunset on the Sea	117
Icy Visit	118
Winter Light	118
Winter Snowstorm	119
Winter Snow	121
By the Lake	122
Tales of Afternoon	122
Each Could Bury Me	123
Sunset Talk	124
Winter	125
The Spider and the Moth	125
Redbird	126
Wildflowers	126
Timberline	127
A Summer Gone	128
Cedar and Oak	129
Standing in the Surf	129
The Bee	130
Winter Wheat	131
Evening	132
The Four Seasons	133
Ivy	134
What I Like	135
I See Beginnings	136
Fossils	136
Rainstorm	137
Wild Southwester	138
Winter Hills	139
What I Want	141
Cool Shade	142
The Riffle	143
Fierce Storm	144
Wild Violets	144
Autumn Prairie	145
I Walk the Hills	146
Seashore	147
Morning	148
The River Mushroom	149
Mountain Talk	149

The Bee and I Can Share	150
Leaves of Autumn	151
Shades of Green	152
Country Snowstorm	153
Thunderstorm	154
Cold Twilight Walk	155
The Deep Woods	156
The Snake	157
Mountain View	158
September Caterpillars	159
The Owl	160
Sandy Seashore	161
Dawn	161
Calling	163
River Flat Cottonwoods	164
The Autumn Cottonwood	165
Sunlight	165
The Empty Land	167
Raindrop	168
The Squirrels	169
Shades of Night	170
Swiss Alps	170
Redbird and Babies	171
Nature Talk	173
April	174
Two Baker's Dozen	175
Cold Winter Woods	175
Warm Spring Morning	176
Trees Fringe Bright	177
First Frost	177
Where Pigeons Home	178
Autumn Hue	178
No Mercy	179
Blackbirds	180
Rose Bouquet	181
A Country Freeze	183
Early Morning	184
The Plush Green Forest	185
Saturday Morning Sun	186
Moon over Manhattan	186
Rising Sun	187
A Butterfly	188

Snowflakes	189
Day	190
Spring	190
Into the Deep	191
First Light	191
The Way It Is	192
Case Won	193
Summer Downpour	193
The Sea Wave	195
The Desert	196
A Bright Winter Day	197
Deep Canyon	199
Spring Sunset	200
How the Sun and Moon Rose	200

Love

Thanksgiving Morning	203
The Facade	204
I Shall Remember	205
Leave Me Something	206
I Heard Sweet Music	207
Together	208
The Twain Shall Meet	208
First Meeting	209
I Took the Moonlight	210
The Darkened Night to Day	211
Pretty Eyes	212
Hidden Love	213
A Life to Make	213
She Was Gone	214
Love Me Now	215
The Sun Rose	215
If I Could Be a Pretty Flower	216
Too Risky	217
The Purpose	218
Near but Far	218
Panic	219
I Need You	220
A Note in the Wind	221
Cupid	222
Sensual Curves	223

Valentines	224
Sophia	225
We Met in National City	226
Fantasy	227
With Someone	227
Mother's Love	228

Spiritual

He Answered My Prayer	231
Throughout My Passing Day	232
A Cathedral Tune	232
Time's Sting	233
What's Real in the World	234
Conjecture	236
The Rainbow	236
Until Heaven	237
No Compromise	238
Down the Deep Earth	238
Sunday Church	239
The Bible	240
Find Eden	240
He Let Me Go	241
Is There Still a Paradise	242
God Is Merciful	243
Each Night Will Dawn	244
Death	245
Heaven Is Everything	247
Ode to Ruth	248
Christmas 1979	249
The Unbeliever	250
Listen to My Heart	251
The Temple of God	252
Passion Fall	252
I Walked the Woods	253
Prayer	254
The Will	254
Christmas	255
Young in Jesus	256
We Must Move On	256
Questions for My Angel	257
I Know	258

A Book of Life	259
Spirit, Soul, and Body	259
Webs of Love	260
Take Me	261
Zoe — Life	262
Love Song for Jesus	263
God's People	264
God Has the Answer	265
Paul	266
Glory	267
Faithful Faith	267
Temporal World	269
Faith	269
Christmas Eve and Morning	270
The Other Side	271
God's Agape	272
A Longing Quest	273
An Hour Ago	274
Judgment	274
Gentle in the Night	275
Two Worlds	275
Passion by Itself	276
Flight	277
I Will Not Judge You	278
Into Heaven	278
Grace	279
Life's Walk	280

Life

Kansas River viaduct, Manhattan, Kansas.

THAT OL' BRIDGE

That ol' bridge across the river
In wintertime was cold
It was built back in the thirties
And now is getting old

That ol' bridge would remember me
The times we spent alone
Our sharing of my early teens
Its squeak and creak and moan

My hollow tread upon its arch
Still echoes there today
And it would know my sweep of step
As if 'twere yesterday

KANSAS DUST

I came from roots of Kansas dust
In God is where I put my trust
I kept the faith, put on its gown
In the country and in the town

I cannot understand the hate
That I see spawn and circulate
It must be from another dust
That lost its love and lost its trust

I still hear echo that far year
He taught me faith and what to trust
The day the long winds took my fear
Of going back to Kansas dust

BICYCLE RIDE

It was a day of summer heat
My legs were pumping with a beat
The sky was dreaming brilliant blue
The clouds awake were drifting through

I looked to distant hill and sky
To fields of wheat much closer by
There snaked a river in between
More in knowing than what I'd seen

The far woods marched on its left flank
Without a drill or breaking rank
And overran the flat's carefree
In plumes as far as eyes could see

SUBURB MORNING

The morning broke with vigor
The shadows laughing long
The grass was stringing dewdrops
The birds were deep in song

The day was fast unfolding
The sun was arching high
Life would be a dreadful thing
Without a morning sky

COUNTRY MORNING

The hawk was at its hunting
The quail called to its mate
The crow was at its cawing
The squirrel in hot debate

It was a country morning
With bacon on my plate
My folks were at the table
Talking about the state

LAS VEGAS

From out of soft and brilliant skies
I soared in winds the eagle flies
From its perspective I looked down
On vast mosaic desert town

Las Vegas came on Boeing's wings
A cabbie filled me in on things
My eyes were struck almost blind
The tawdry lights, the "out of mind"

I roamed casinos with an eye
Why would patrons all odds defy?
And go-for-broke with hopeless schemes
When in the end it's broken dreams

This country boy from prairie hills
Was used to folks with little frills
Easy smiles and inbred honesty
Neighborly hospitality

But here beneath a false-hoped air
Where insolence and tempers flare
Where people shove and people haste
Where dealers show a face of paste

I met a waitress with a smile
In this vast sea she was an isle
Of fresh flowers, among the few
That like themselves for what they do

WHEN NATURE CALLS TO ME

I like the warmth of a spring day
Without a thing
To disturb the mind or anxious the heart
So I can hear the ring
When Nature calls to me

I like to wend, like yesterdays
Without a stint
Of any care, free as all the angels
To feel the way God meant
When Nature calls to me

GHETTO MORNING

Mother and children sleep
Touched by the sun's first rays
Through a dusty window
And webs of lazy days

In the kitchen a rat
Sniffs at the rotting air
Dishes crowd a dirty sink
In a pile of despair

THE OPEN-FACED SPINNER

It was a clear, hot summer day
When Everett, Ray, and I
Went fishing on the Blue River
Beneath an endless bright sky

Ray and I laughed and stomped our feet
Beneath a rustling cottonwood
When we saw Ev's new rod and reel
We knew were cheap and no good

We shook our heads looking at the
Clear thread line, light rod, and spinner
We watched as he put on a hook
And tiny split-shot sinker

He raised the rod, and with a flip
He sailed the line at least half-way
Or more across the wide river
He caught fish all through the day

That night we each gave Everett
The $9.99 hot deal
To buy us each by next weekend
That magical rod and reel

To my good friends, Ray Drapeau and Everett Parsons. This was the first open-faced spinning reel Ray and I had ever seen. It was cheap and made of plastic, but it revolutionized the fishing reel.

A BROTHER

I have a brother in the hills
Above all else he likes the spills
Of Nature in the bluestem glow
And all the sun can touch below

He likes it there beside a lake
He likes the shade the oak trees make
With his touch, the wildflowers sing
The birds come in, to feed, awing

He strives for sounds out far and near
He brings them in where all can hear
It's in the broken hills of green
Out where the blooms of grace are seen

THE OLD HOUSE

The old house was in need of paint
The fence, repair
The old garage door hung ajar
Dangling from its weight

There was no grass in the front yard
The plants were browning
The old house was slowly breaking
The barren grounds cracking

A new family bought the place
Repaired the fence
Put a coat of paint on the house
Fixed up around complete

From out of the house came music
People singing
The place just needed some fixing
And celebrating

SHE WORE A ROSE

She wore a rose
Upon each cheek
She wore a smile
That all men seek

I do not know
A time or place
There was not joy
Upon her face

When her blue eyes
Would look at me
I felt the stir
Of ecstasy

SHE WORE A FROWN

She wore a frown
Wrinkled from care
Her years of hate
Had put them there

I knew her long
Before she died
Never a smile
She could have lied

Never knew her
When things were right
Seems such a shame
She wore such spite

THE RIFLE SHOT

In the summer outside, alone
I walked among the shades of night
The moon was full and rising high
The treetops gleamed a silver sheen
The land was deep in ghostly sleep
The pine was glowing shades of green

A sycamore's white limbs of bone
Looked eerie in the dim moonlight
Then sharp I heard a rifle shot
Racketing across a still sky
Fading off into the far hills
I felt a chill and death close by

NINETEEN NINETY

They, Sammy Davis, Irene Dunne,
Ava Gardner, Rex Harrison,
Mary Martin, Barbara Stanwyck,
And more, went home to God this year

Many more have passed on before
That filled my life with cinema
When I was young and just a boy
They gave me the American dream

Their deaths bring my mortality,
My life here into perspective
And bring down another curtain
On the glamorous silver screen

THE DROWNING

In the summer with my parents
We drove out to a nearby lake
The water was blue, calm, and clear
It was like glass, without a wake

On a far beach people gathered
Around a body on the ground
They milled around in a circle
Beseeching God for just a sound

My limp heart was badly shaken
It was impossible to revive
A future for the little boy
Who looked about my age of five

SAN DIEGO

The mountains rim
Purple hem
San Diego Bay

The roadways trestle
Homes nestle
Along the way

The harbor lights
Candlelights
A nightly host

The car lights stream
Glowing gleam
Along the coast

The islands sweep
Ghostly sleep
Against the sky

In the morning glow
Misty low
The sea gulls cry

Great hulls corrode
Ships unload
Beside the quay

The ships detail
Setting sail
Down to the sea

The day's gray light
Filters bright
A sunny noon

The people sing
Blossoms bring
A sundry tune

WHEN THE MOVIE'S OVER

In crowded push
Its patrons rush
The theater door
Unbottled now
Outside they pour

Then fanning out
They run about
Beneath the stars
Where headlights stream
From racing cars

FISHING MAN

The old man said to his neighbor
"You ought to know by now
For you seem to go off fishing
More than you ever plow

"What bait would be good for fishing
What nature now provides
What natural food is abundant
What moon, what winds, what tides"

"I'd say a minnow would be good
Hooked right to splash and squirm
Yet, if God said I could have but one
I think I'd choose a worm"

My children, Susan, Marcia, and Richard.

MY CHILDREN

This is to all my children
Beloved more than day
This feeling that I feel
Will ever with me stay

I hope you judge me tenderly
On flaws that made you sad
Accept my better moments
And overlook my bad

Each of you calls up feelings
That only you can call
If all could feel as I do
Then love would take us all

My brothers — Don, Jim, Earl, Art — and me.

THE OLD MEYERS PLACE

On both creek sides, ground, high and low,
Between the hill and river flow
My father farmed, fixed up around,
Conquered the weeds, prepared the ground

Laid disc to sod and rake to grass
Put out the cows to hill and pass
Horses to work at early light
Put them to barn before the night

We gave the good old place some zing
We made her hum and made her sing
Then one by one we went away
Now others there must work its clay

NIGHT FISHING

Outside I went on soundless feet
Light as a summer dream
Into the heart of deepest night
And to a riffled stream

I tossed my bait out in the stream
Just out beyond my sight
Out where the pool looked black and deep
Below the rushing white

I felt the loose line tighten up
With a hard pull and swing
Then there was a splash of fury
And my heartbeat racing

MOTHER'S FUNERAL

I took one last look
At her still face
For a familiar trace
It was not there
She was welded stone
Of skin and bone
In silk cocoon

The cemetery words
Went most unheard
As the people stirred
Around the grave
I stood there alone
Glad to have known
Her kind of love

With Jana, December 1982, at the Bascom home.

WANDERLUST

I have an impulse somewhere deep
That goads me even when I sleep
To wipe my feet of Kansas dust
And do my thing in wanderlust

Take the seed from what I lack
And scattered bring the flowers back
Forget all obligations stale
Close down the shop, and stop the mail

Let the wind through ages steal
But can I do this thing I feel
My duties are ingrained in me
And leaving feels like blasphemy

THE OLD NOTE

The thin old man
Was very poor
Alone
Lived in a shack
On a dirt floor

They found him dead
In his homespun
Old watch
And a shoe box
Tied in a ribbon

A worn old note
In the box gave
Millions
To the old man
He could not read

A DAY FOR FISHING

The sky up high was held in blue
The sun was bright and glaring through
Great ships of clouds were on the run
Casting shadows before the sun

The winds were blowing off the rim
A light gleamed on the bluestem
In shades of praise the morning sent
A day for fishing, and I went

THE QUESTER

The sky is awash with moonlight
The quester is looking at night
He mingles with a kindred crowd
In merriment a while

Out on the floor a black-eyed girl
Enchantingly dances a whirl
She gives to him a knowing glance
Then flaunts a flippant smile

THE OLD MAN AND THE MIRROR

The old man looked in a mirror
At his gray, thinning hair
With his young, stout heart he looked back
At the boy standing there

Before him there was his childhood
To him the most profound
Experiences of his long life
He waited for a sound

Of childhood to his aged ears
And then he wondered how
The things important to him then
Were not important now

A bitter taste stuck in his mouth
Looking into the dim
Eyeing the best part of his life
Always there behind him

Then he listened and when God spoke
He saw a hand release
Its dark grip upon the mirror
And at last he found peace

FATHER'S DEATH
(March 1963)

A recognition came to his eye
Then there came a puzzlement
He tried to figure who I was
With a look of wonderment

Helplessly I watched as he then
Moved eyes around the room
Searching, soundlessly questioning
With eyes that looked at doom

Then came the thrash of dying throe
The vast and final breach
Fingers strained for something out of reach
Or was it out of reach?

He trembled down and then was still
Stone eyes took on a stare
The struggle in the breast stopped
The fight for breathing air

I stood there in the silent time
Almost in disbelief
They closed his eyes, I closed death's door
Then opened the door of grief

Martha Pearl (Branick) Ross and Herbert Thomas Cleveland Ross.

MOTHER'S DEATH
(August 1979)

I stood there stunned by the process
Of my mother's dying
I felt a chill down in my bones
Much too cold for crying

In minutes it was all over
Her eyes shut, Spirit free
The doctor did a final check
But her shell was empty

I walked out down a dark hallway
To an outside of light
A brassy sun filled up the sky
And squinted my eyesight

From out of a distant tower
I heard sirens screaming
A tree was casting dark shadows
And the birds were singing

HE SMILED AT ME

When I walked into the cafe
The old man smiled at me
I sat by him at the counter
He welcomed me graciously

He treated me as a friend
And I a stranger from afar
He made me wonder why it is
That we are the way we are

Many I've met will never speak
And if I speak they turn away
I liked the old man's attitude
He left me with a nicer day

THE OLD WOMAN

The stern old woman looked at me
Out of marble raised eyes
With a sly, mean-looking frown
Frozen in deep despise

It must have taken years to imbed
The wrinkles in her skin
For those crag-like grooves will never
Now unwrinkle again

The old woman was long past change
Now deep chiseled in stone
The years had worn her hate so deep
The Angels took her throne

Garden of the Gods, Colorado Springs, Colorado.

FRONTIER SPIRIT

My frontier spirit stirs me deep
Should I stay safe, or should I leap
Out to an unfamiliar dawn
Go out and see what spurs me on

I get the urge to cross the sea
Like the priest's call to deity
I want to see, I want to feel
Before old age can turn its wheel

TO THE SEA

I wanted to, when I went to the sea
It was in my heart for me to see
The ships were docked, masts pointed high
Like fingered needles in the sky

The sea, my dreams awaited me there
The hands were signing, but my mother's prayer
Was too strong for me, sea, or ship
And I went home with a curled lip

Harold Ross in San Diego.

BOYHOOD SUMMER

It was a long boyhood summer
From light to dark in happy play
The days were life unquenchable
And then the summer went away

Time brought on another summer
I looked, but could not find the boys
Summers, I learned, are not the same
And to a toy box went my toys

YESTERDAYS

The good old days are with the star
Yesterdays' winds and clouds afar
In clipper sails and mountain snow
They rest out where the good boys go

Beyond the land, beyond the sea
They are beyond where eyes can see
They are in time and out of mind
Where people look and never find

NIGHTFALL ON THE FARM

I stopped to look at stars up high
To watch the dark fall from the sky
It blacked the woods where birds abound
And grayed a meadow closer by

It rained ink down without a sound
Like raindrops falling to the ground
It coated trees that fringed skies stark
And dimmed the fields and fences round

A rabbit raced and left no mark
A whippoorwill called from the dark
It sang out from its grassy lair
To brush where creatures hide and hark

Then the moon rose opal and fair
And lit a haystack's tawny hair
From out our window, light stretched a hand
And took my own on front porch stair

POOCH

I was a small boy
When Dad brought the puppy home
Without a name

He was my mate
Through the times we were awake
In light or dark

We were a team
Broke new trails in woods out far
In mist or clear

One day Pooch died
Dad said, "Bury the poor soul,
On yonder hill"

A MOTHER AND SON

The mother raised a house of boys
Filled up her home with children's noise
One day she pushed one off her lap
And sent him off by ship to sea
In winds to shores of slope and tree
From harbor lights and parchment map
He plowed a trough of watery wake
Conquered the land for Mother's sake
Dreamed his dreams, asleep and awake
That sparked an ember in his soul
Pursued the ring the church bells toll
And heard the beat of drumbeat roll

Like all good boys his heart was rent
When Mother asked that he repent
He went for liberty instead
Where guns and death in fields meet
He found that love knows no defeat
And found the ground had all turned red
Hallowing it in freedom won
That brought the wind and brought the sun
Back to a mother and a son
Together now they always stand
Steadfast, in sky, on sea, and land
America and England

THE FLOOD

Raindrops cast down to make a crowd
They raced into a river flow
That overran to make a flood
And swept the ground all in its way

It scooped up earth and ran amuck
It rooted out debris and trees
That went off swiftly in the roar
As the backwater filtered mud

Rain dispersed more troops in the night
That took a bridge here, a house there
And left behind bare beaten fields
Like Sherman's march to the sea

GONE

If I could only hear her now
Her voice and singing that is still
If I could take her flowers pink
Picked fresh from off the pastured hill

To look again upon her face
Now frozen like the crusted snow
To smell again the baking bread
Now gone with spats and calico

If I could feel again the dirt
With bare feet on that sun-warm lane
I'd think 'twas Heaven here for me
With the fragrance of summer rain

SUNSET RUN

Racing on a swell of the sea
A merchant ship along the key
Looks dim and vague before its run
Between the cape and setting sun

The ship lifts in the flaming sea
Then only masts are left to see
They lift again before the sun
Then down together as but one

I look as far as eyes can leap
The ship is gone upon the deep
Though saying it has sunk would be
I think, presumptuous of me

MY FATHER'S DEATH

My father's death
Was like a stone
Into the water
Sinking past my sight

Only we close to him
Can still see the waves
The rings disappearing
Beyond his grave

THEN WHERE

If all be fair in love and war
If means can justify the end
If good be a part of evil
Then where is certainty

If most men are not strong enough
To deny themselves anything
If passion controls the body
Then where is serenity

THE OLD WOMAN
AND THE NURSING HOME

The old woman
Was sitting on the ground
Her head was down, looking frightened,
Her eyes were at the point of tears

In the distance
Stood a bleak nursing home
When I spoke to her, she stood up
With a blank look of someone lost

I asked her name
And could I be of help
She said, "I lost off my parents
They will be mad if they're not home

"It's right in there
On the fence below the gate
Out the pasture, and in the creek
They want for me to wait the house"

I took her back
To the brick nursing home
I felt a traitor, but she smiled
With some doubts written on her brow

THE ROLLER SKATER

Out on his skates
Faster than the wind
He raced around the corners,
Legs flying, thrusting in a bend

He then is seen
Through other skaters
Whirling like a dust devil
Across dirt fields and cockleburs

Who is that boy
With his father's pride
And his mother's derring-do
He flaunts to all with his glide

TIME'S GRIP

People do not
Belong to people
But yesterday belongs
To yesterday's time
Nobody has time
For ticking time has us
In a clock's grip

If we could have
Met yesterday
Or when I was young
Had yesterday met us
On even terms
But yesterday is not
And I am not

THE WRITTEN WORD

I like to paint with written words
To catch on paper sights and sounds
Bring out the fragrant taste in lines
That all may touch familiar grounds

I like to brush with strokes that glow
The painting wide in scope and sweep
My hope is when the work's complete
You find it's breathless, find it's deep

I like to feel my spirit soar
It's worth the work of nightly hours
So I search out the distant dales
With my pen to paint more flowers

JUST FOR HER SAKE

There will not ever
Be another
To give me feelings
Like my mother

They are forever
To stir me deep
Where the music plays
And heartbeats leap

I once wanted her
Never to die
But how she suffered
And so did I

I prayed that she die
Just for her sake
Dear God I hope not
Not for my sake

THE TYRANT

She was a mean tyrant
In her own little realm
Of herself and husband
Ruling with an iron mouth

At times you could hear her
Harsh across the dirt field
Berating the poor wretch
Who never spoke a word

He had failed as a man
Early in the marriage
She took his upper hand
Now she beats him with it

AN OLD VACANT HOUSE

It was night, a cloud-like fine mist
Was drifting on the floor
The moonlight was busy working
Down an old battered door

The frogs were croaking in the fog
Disturbing marsh and shore
Then came to ears a silencing
Above the brushy roar

The window casings were empty
Glass broken on the ground
Mystery shrouds the crumbling house
And wild growth around

There was nothing there of value
It long ago was found
The place had lost its soul and life
Along with any sound

THE TRAIN

When a boy in bed at night
I could hear
In the far distance a train
From out of the midnight prairie

I could hear the whistle blow
Hear the click
Of the iron wheels on track
Hear her chugging taking on coal

Visions would dance in my mind
Soft velvet
Framed red the plush parlor car
People lounged in their rich attire

Steam streamed by the windowpane
In a mist
Black prairie was but a blur
But no one there would take notice

The whistle enchantingly
Was calling
Echoing down the night sky
Rushing off into the deep dark

The clang of bell was a ring
In my mind
As the sound disappeared
Into the silence of my room

BACK TO YOU

You both conceived and put me here
Then you, Dad, were first to leave
And then you, Mother, left me too
With nought but time to grieve

And now I can hardly see you
Or feel your many ways
You come and you go like dim ghosts
In dreams of yesterdays

Memories don't seem to provide
The one with all to do
So maybe death is what I'll need
To take me back to you

Clarks Creek, upstream about a quarter of a mile from where we lived.

Harold Ross on Queenie.

CLARKS CREEK

In late winter out in the snow
When I was a little boy
The sun was glaring, bright and warm
A day for play and joy

I wandered to the nearby creek
And toddled down the bank
A sled was resting on the ice
It beckoned and I sank

Into the water through the ice
I fought the current's sweep
In vain I splashed and deeper sank
Down in the blossomed deep

It was my Guardian Angel
That sent a message stark
And it brought to me a brother
Who pulled me from the dark

WITH HIM WENT HER WILL TO TRUST

The woman was always alone
I used to see her around some
But seldom see her anymore
I think she grieves behind her door
At her long ago investment

I heard when she was pert and young
She fell in love and then he left
What he called love was only lust
And with him went her will to trust
Nor would she ever try again

Someone should have tried to tell her
There are times when you need someone
If just to say look over there
When there is something you can share
And someone who will always care

THE FUNERAL

Oh dear mercy
It was the day of her funeral
And I was stunned clear to the bone
How could such gloom close in and surround me
This feeling of doom should never be

Heaven forbid
I thought, this must be a depraved dream
As I walked into the dim church
Eerie organ music added to the smart
Of woe that stirred me deep in my heart

Goodness gracious
There surely was a better way
To tell someone you love goodbye
That somehow gave you a feeling of joy
Like going home when I was a boy

SHE HAD NO SECRETS

She was beautiful
Thoughtful and kind
Rare qualities
In one to find

"I have no secrets,"
She told me there
To believe her
Was only fair

My, how wonderful
It sure would be
To have that feeling
Inside of me

A PRETTY LADY

I walked into a smoke-filled room
There was no glow of candlelight
Nor shadows playing on the walls
A place where people came with night

The patrons there were having fun
Before the night in evening-glow
She with a friend and I alone
A lady that I did not know

We met and at her table talked
With jukebox music in the air
I found in her a kindred soul
And with me, she and evening share

Our thoughts and spirits were akin
Our poetry, the way we are
I felt the stir of something deep
As if 'twere kisses from afar

San Diego Bay.

SAN DIEGO BAY

Along the boardwalk shore
Along the purple way
Along the shipyard's dock
And lights on dappled bay

Before the vast Pacific
Before the deep unknown
Before the masted sail
The bay to blossoms blown

I MIGHT DEMURE

Despair is mild to what I feel
I freeze alone the nightly air
Before me time forever steals
Wealth is nothing if you compare

So give me breath when I'm asleep
Don't take in death what can endure
And if I die please do not weep
For at the last I might demure

THE OLD MILL

I remember the old grain mill
On the road into town
Between the hill and riverbank
That man or time tore down

Beside the mill was an old bridge
That once crossed the river
Now also gone like rising mist
From the falling water

The only thing that's left there now
Is a small riffled fall
Across the Smoky River
Where once the dam stood tall

THE SKULL

A human skull lay half buried in sand
Bleached white it stared with empty eyes
A hot breeze worked on a creosote bush
Beneath a sun that scorched the skies

A bullet hole had pierced the weathered skull
Where life was suddenly ended
A buzzard swung loops watching from the sky
Where patience would be rewarded

The Mogollon Rim and piñons would know
Whose bones were laid out at its feet
The Sonoran Desert can more than show
One old skull cleaned by its heat

A LOVING THOUGHT

I had a loving thought today
This and my heart divide
This, the land, the sea, the sky
And all the cosmos wide

To touch the old and lonely
Help wipe from them a frown
See if there can be a smile
Before their hearts run down

THE WIFE

She put away her Barbie doll
She thought it right to give her all
To be a loving, caring wife
To just grow up, get on with life

If she regretted her new place
I saw no frown upon her face
If there were pains within her day
She hid them somewhere far away

I WANT TO GO

I want to go, when young, in time
Go back past grief and back the years
Where lips are sweet and life sublime
Where when I cry they're joyful tears
And youth ignores approaching years

I want to go a country road
Where moonlight gleams a star-struck sky
Where heartstrings play a poet's ode
Where boys place girls mountains high
And that respect will never die

I want to go where lovers side
Where I can hear the sea gulls' cries
Where South Sea winds and shores beside
Where each dawn golds in brilliant skies
Is this too much to ask for eyes

Summer evening.

EVENING BRINGS ALL THINGS HOME

I look at life more often now
Eyeing the encroachment of years
There is a point not far ahead
When it will all come to an end

I see everything change and yet
I see everything stay the same
Now death seems faint and far away
And I still long for yesterday

Then from out of an arching sky
Within a soft, caressing wind
I hear a whispering in the leaves
That evening brings all things home

A DAY SPLITTING WOOD

Saturday I liked a leisure bed
But I was splitting wood instead
"The winter's close" my father said
"Split wood until there is no more"
I had no vote on this grim chore
A stack of wood above my head
It hid from sight a nearby shed
And fringed a gray and chilly sky
I wondered why prepare for snow
With better places I could go
My axe would bite and never know
That I listened to every swing
To every swish and crack and ring
I know the far woods heard each blow
Each echoed thud till twilight glow

LIFE'S STRUGGLES

In life we reach for
Something out of hand
And we search out far
Past sea and land

We even search out
Where the cosmos go
To the other far suns
Look high and low

The answer is here
To trust without sight
God is our freedom
His word is our light.

THE MERRY-GO-ROUND

The people circle
Standing all around
They are now watching
The merry-go-round

The horses and kids
Are half riding up
And half riding down
On the merry-go-round

The music's loud sound
Is now piping up
And then piping down
On the merry-go-round

The children all laugh
A delightful sound
When whirling by
On the merry-go-round

The people circle
Standing all around
They are still watching
The merry-go-round

TOUGH COWBOY

A cowboy rode into the town
He wore two guns, low and tied down
Came from the west, low desert sand
Out of the sun, Apache land

Tied his horse to the hitching rail
It stood three-legged, switching tail
Beat dust from his clothes with his hat
Then walked up to the Feline Cat

He threw open the bat-wing doors
Like sea waves thrown against the shores
Went to the bar and ordered rye
And looked around with one closed eye

Four cowboys cringed deep in the room
The tawdry saloon felt like doom
When they thought he reached for a gun
The four raced out to get some sun

THE GOOD OLD DAYS

Each day at dawn
The man walked out
In mind about
To the far woods

Each day at dusk
He rode his eyes
To long lost skies
And distant hills

Each day was full
Mind busying
Remembering
The good old days

As for the times
He went through bad
His old mind had
Amnesia

ROBERT E. LEE

What knowledge I have of Lee
Came from books of many pages
His love for state and people stands
Forever down the ages

I suffered too his grim ordeals
Shared the triumphs, the anguished tears
I died his death at Appomattox
Felt his pride the post-war years

I took and shook his kindly hand
Admired the traits we all adore
To know him was a privilege
He is a man forevermore

Kristin Smith.

A PONY FOR KRISTIN

There is a sweet lass named Kristin
Who has a pretty grin
And like most any other Ross
She bears a harmless cross

The Rosses here, or far apart
Have ponies in their hearts
Passed down the years like an heirloom
Ponies, like flowers, bloom

From out of the Virginia grass
Come ponies through the pass
Don't be surprised when on that day
A pony comes to stay

NATURE WILL DECIDE

I've walked along the ravaged earth
From here to there across its girth
It is the winds, it is the rains
The sun, the moon, mountains and plains

The arid lands, the boundless seas
Forests, rivers, the air, disease
The droughts, hunger, fire and heat
The storms, the floods, ice, snow and sleet

In the end nature will decide
What sanctuaries can we hide?
Its elements rule you and I,
How we shall live, how we shall die

WINTER STAGECOACH RUN

The fallen snow was drifted deep
Along the slopes where shadows sleep
The twilight sun beyond all sight
Brushed pink a sky of turning night

The mountain sheer loomed vast and gray
The slopes and cliffs were through with day
The valley flats were growing dim
The scene was ghostly, cold, and grim

The snow draped fir limbs like white sleeves
And hung on houses over eaves
It laid its cotton blanket round
And over growth upon the ground

Down beaten tracks filled up with flakes
Along the white of hidden brakes
Four frosty horses were stamping down
From off the mountain into town

The horses pulled into a light
From out a window shining bright
The stagecoach gleamed with lamp lit gold
And sudden welcome from the cold

Farm east of Manhattan, Kansas.

FARM NOSTALGIA

From out of the prairies
And the broken hills
I can hear the fairies
When nostalgia spills

From out of the valleys
And the bottom soils
I can see the oak trees
And yesterday's toils

From out of the making
Of a cast iron pan
I can smell the baking
Of bread, golden tan

From out of my senses
And thoughts turning cold
I long for the fences
And farms, growing old

THE FARMHOUSE

Beneath the hill
Stands a house of stone
On a knoll, in groves
Of oak, alone

The old farmhouse
Stands silent and still
It is watching time
Beneath the hill

GOOD DAYS AND NIGHTS

From out of our days
Let there be a rose
With all of its fame
Without its woes

From out of our nights
Let there be a star
With all of its charm
Yet not so far

SATURDAY MORNING

From out of the house I could hear
The sound of music in the air
Through the yard, and the brush
Out into the fields and distance

I heard Mom, singing and playing
The piano with joyful hands
Pop was at some last-minute chores
I was awaiting our trip to town

Mom's music was festive, no cares
Although, Lord knows, we had our share
But nothing could keep our hopes down
When we had our music and town

Ixtapa, Mexico.

MY BREW IS LIFE

I drink a brew not made in vats
I drink the sea, the sky, the land
Not all the liquor in the Earth
Compares at all with my aged brand

I get high on drams of air
Intoxicated by the day
I reel through the rain and snow
When out-of-doors I sometimes sway

There will never be a liquor
Inebriate in better ways
Nor match the potion God stirred up
Who brewed the Earth in seven days

AN EARTH FULL OF HOPE

Out on a morning bike ride
I raced the winds of day
With the beauty of the landscape
It cast my cares away

The sky was held in brilliant glow
Of morning's misty light
The air was calm and fresh and clean
The day was pure delight

The birds were a chorus of music
The crows were in the blue
The horses out, were switching tails
With heads to grass and dew

God had laid a misty finger
Upon the distant slope
And my heart was overflowing
In an Earth full of hope

UP TO THE PASTURE

Our pasture lay above our farm
In broken hills of bluestem grass
That fellowship with rock and brush
And a few seeps with pools below

This was rugged old hill country
But our milk cows took to the grass
Later on in the afternoons
We would bring them in for milking

Finding the cows was a problem
Though one was collared with a bell
That was until we got some help
From Pooch, half mongrel, half sheepdog

Finding the cows became easy
That ol' dog could ferret them out
In minutes Pooch could find those cows
In the brush, slough, or wherever

Dad would point and say, "Get them boy"
And into the brush and pasture
Pooch would take off like a hurled shot
Legs flying, belly low, surging

Like he was hunting for a bone
Taking with him a cloud of dust
In a short time he would then be
Pushing those milk cows to the barn

Nothing reminds me more of then
Than milk cows walking slowly down
A pasture lane, switching their tails
In the light of an afternoon

Our house on Rannells Road.

WINTER MORNING

Beneath the winter morning's bright
The land around was buried white
Snow filled ditches, filled the sloughs
And shadows went from blacks to blues

Out on the porch effaced with snow
I heard the sweep and felt the blow
I looked and found there near a bench
A dusted scoop I used to trench

A tunnel through drifts high and deep
Up to the barn where sides were steep
I opened door to dust and cold
The smell of hay and leather old

Inside by bins and harness racks
Came blades of sunlight through the cracks
And through the pen where my horse blew
Shook her head, and paced anew

I gave her water, a wedge of hay
Shouldered the scoop and quit the day
Went through the snow path and its glare
Into the house and soft warm air

A DYING TRACK

Beside me ran the railroad tracks
On ties and mounds of gray ballast
The sunlight was blinding my eyes
Glowing bright off the top rails

In the far distance I saw the tracks
Merge into one then disappear
As it rounded a hillside curve
In a tail of sun-streaked glow

The roadbed carried an aroma
Of creosote and acrid smell
That took me back to my younger years
When I would walk the railroad tracks

The steel-bolted and spiked-on rails
Wait patiently for the daily
The old track used to hum with trains
Now it dies from a lack of use

THE LITTLE GIRL

She was a little girl
A pretty child
And was lavished with love
By her parents

They, burdened with Earth's cares
Without reason
Would at times snap anger
Toward the child

Then the sad child asked
"Do all grownups
Love you one day
And not the next"

EARLY FISHING

The stars were shining in the night
Like little campfires in the deep
The midnight winds were fast asleep
Before a faint encroaching light

My world seemed dim and far away
Creek waters beckoned by the trees
Where shadows pranced beneath a breeze
And dawn's first light brushed limbs with gray

I went to shallows racing cold
And pitched my fish line in its pool
I watched a mist rise from the cool
I felt a pull, and fish take hold

AN OLD STONE HOUSE

On a dirt road in a clearing of trees
Stood an old stone house all run-down and worn
In that house, stair steps of children were born
They wore old denims with holes at the knees

Each child was blessed with the vigor of youth
They played in the dirt until dark and late
Inside a downed fence with a hanging gate
In a yard of neglect, to tell the truth

Out in the garden were weeds growing wild
That half hid a bucket on an old post
What came from that ground would be small at most
Without much there for a growing child

All that joy and laughter coming from there,
Without a new toy, was love at its best
For in their innocence they all were blessed
God gave them His grace, a handsome share

The children were happy though they were poor
So what if they were all covered with dirt
In their hearts they grew strong without any hurt
And what in life could someone want more

SOME SPICE

I know this couple forlorn and poor
They are down and out with life a bore
It seems there should be more to life
Than every day unceasing strife

Somewhere between the heart and soul
We need to hear the laughter roll
There is a need, when work is done
A need in life for having fun

There is a time for song and night
A time to paint and make things bright
It's right in life to want some spice
With someone else especially nice

SILENCE

What's more silent than a bitter night
When the snow looks blue, but pure white
That even the killer, frigid frost
Wears soundless shoes stalking the lost

Unless it's the silence in the gloom
Always present in a living room
Where the old will nap and never talk
The only sound a ticking clock

DEPRESSED

My heart is depressed and heavy
It's like an empty room
With nothing there of memory
To still my grief and gloom

If I could see a dust mote float
In a blade of sunlight
Through a yesterday's laced curtain
My day would pass through night

A FRIEND IS GONE

The lady, the casket, moved slowly
Through the gate and monument lawn
The people lined around the grave
Gathering together in a ring

To pay respect to her husband
And then the sermon was over
The people parted to their homes
She to a house of memories

It will be hard for her, you know
For not only were they lovers
They were also the best of friends
And no death will separate them

WAITED

I knew a man who waited
Waited so long he died
Waited for what? I had thought
When out and on a ride

Not twenty paces, there he sat
From Highway 24
In the heat or cold in his chair
Not twenty paces from his door

Then came that day he sat no more
Waited so long he died
To wait and wait would be a curse
If nothing else were tried

SCIENTIFIC REPORT

The results of a new study
Were broadcast on the news last night
Compiled by noted scientists
From the best universities

A study of the universe
On hydrogen and outer space
Galaxies, black holes, stars, comets
And things I cannot remember

It was a study overseas
Financed by a grant to scholars
The results were inconclusive
Millions spent in the name of peace

They did agree to use one word
To describe space — it would be Light
God could have saved them time and money
The Bible, Genesis 1-3

EARLY MORNING FRONTIER TOWN

In the vast distant prairie land
The dawn was gray, the clouds were tinged
With light now fanned across the sky
Below the hills the darkness cringed
And raced in shadows on the fly

The light raced past the gullies
Past the quiet and sleeping town
Dawn's first hint made a rooster crow
Who turned his dusty regal crown
Toward the golden sunlight glow

A screen door slammed and split the calm
A rusted pump was quickly drawn
Its water gushed into a pail
And broke the solitude of dawn
Out West on the Oregon Trail

A MINISKIRT
(Early 1960s)

The dawn's first light was turning gray
It dimly lit the gloomy scene
A light from a lone windowpane
Shone from Ray's house as I pulled up

The light turned off, as Ray walked out
With fishing gear and fishing pack
I then drove off on down the street
As the landscape took on more gray

Driving through the city we saw
Walking the street a pretty girl,
There were no other people in sight,
Swishing her hips, with a smile

The nymph was almost naked
And that was what I noticed first
A low-cut blouse, shapely hips wrapped
In a black mini miniskirt

I looked at Ray, he looked at me
When she put more swing in her walk
I started to turn at the corner
To take the car around the block

Ray said, "No! No! Don't turn this car
We are going fishing and that's it"
And I said, "But" and he said, "No!"
So we went fishing, with our thoughts

DAWN AT THE BAY

The mooring lights are shining
The mists off seas are climbing
Houses light up across the bay
On silent waters far away

Sea gulls on wharfs are cuddling
Deckhands by fires are huddling
A foghorn blasts one ghostly yawn
And then one more to greet the dawn

MY MOTHER

I can't stop the tears
But, she was worth it, even the grief
Now seems mild as I remember
My younger years with her

And I try to sleep
But I hear the sounds of the city
Racketing off down the dark nights
Into the luring lights

KANSAS CITY V.A. HOSPITAL

The building antiseptic clean
Where patients bed with hope and pains
Outside the solemn grasses sleep
And border concrete walks and lanes

I sat a bench on V.A. lawn
And looked at sky and treetops trace
Beneath stacked banks of whipped-cream clouds
Along the hills that fringed like lace

Beside the sun-streaked silver rays
Through purple clouds crowned with sunlight
A steel-meshed curtain of rainfall
Walked the distance it hid from sight

GOING NOWHERE AT ALL

From out of the darkness of nights
There rides upon the rails
A call that, an impulse, excites
And echoes sea and sails

I hear the sounds of distant train
Its whistled sorcery
Shrilling down the midnight plain
Making its call to me

Come run romantic mystic line
I hear another call
Of clickety-click and lonely whine
Going nowhere at all

EXCLUDED

We select our society
Then close the door to entry
In this circle we share our woe,
Our joy, and keep the status quo

I've known the pain of exclusion
Guilty of it for no reason
I now apologize to all
That I excluded with a wall

Nature

Twin Sycamores, upstream from Tuttle Cove, Tuttle Creek Lake.

TWIN SYCAMORES

Near a cold stream
Sycamores dream
Of days gone by

The twins stately
Fringe sedately
Along the sky

The brake runs wild
Like a swift child
Up to their door

The white limbs bend
Before the wind
Then clap for more

The grasses shine
Shadows design
Without a sound

The old leaves crunch
The low brush bunch
Upon the ground

The leaves rustle
The winds bustle
Below the rim

I sense a thrill
Along the hill
Could it be Him

THE UNDECIDED LEAF

High in a tree a leaf breaks free
To slowly rock its way to ground
It lies there curled all alone
And listens for a kindred sound

The undecided leaf lies still
Then a wind moves it like a mouse
Helter-skelter across the grass
And puts it home against the house

TUMBLEWEEDS

I stood alone and faced the wind
I watched it sail across the grass
Like swelling waves from depths within
That raced for shores from off the sea
In the distance a skirmish line
Was moving in fast formation
Tumbleweeds searching for cover
By the thousands had been dispersed
Except for those against the fence
Others flew by and disappeared

DARK BEFORE THE DAWN

It is the dark before the dawn
The time of night with darkest on
Where depths are deep and sight is feel
And rushing tides of shade now steal

The stars like candles in the sky
Come down to Earth before they die
Along the fringe of darkened night
Where winds of dawn blow out each light

THE CRICKET

What makes a cricket, cricket
What makes him want to hide
Why leave the grass and sunny noon
Why hunt a home inside

But Heaven to a cricket
His ultimate desire
Is to play a violin
Close to an autumn fire

TUTTLE SUNSET

An eagle swoops
Last minute loops
In winds up high

The long grass bends
Before the winds
In waves awry

The treetops trace
A leafy lace
Along the sky

The hills turn pink
A golden wink
And then a sigh

Sunlight glitters
Twilight fritters
A dim reply

Disturbingly
Regrettably
It all passed by

MORNING CLOUDS

I drove east toward Topeka
Beneath vast clouds like towels awry
In old washtubs of soapy suds
Thrown across a washboard sky

Through the Flint Hills on the highway
I looked at bluestem plush and green
At morning painting far hills blue
Beyond lit isles of golden sheen

I saw the sunlight shining through
Large white banked clouds in silver splays
Clouds like wrung-out dampened bed sheets
Stacked high from out of yesterdays

A shady nook near Tuttle Creek Lake.

A SHADY NOOK

The trees ring
Ivies cling
A shady nook
A lake dreams
Water gleams
Through where I look

Squirrels fly
Oak leaves die
Along the ground
Shadows sway
Monarchs play
Midst Nature's sound

HOT SUMMER DAY

I rode beside
A railroad track
Its shining rails
Were gleaming back

The track lay dead
And off its feet
Upon a bed
Of burning heat

The heat waves rose
In queer short tails
And shimmered with
The dancing rails

ALONG THE BROKEN HILLS

The autumn woods' color
The paint of artist spills
The long winds gently sweep
Along the broken hills
With a contract to keep

The sumac splashes red
The dogwood brushes rust
The grass is sleeping gold
In its last throes to dust
From a summer gone old

THE WINDOWPANE

The windowpane was fast asleep
Until it heard the pelting sweep
Of wind and snow upon its glass
It faced against the winter blow
And watched the storm stack deeper snow

It watched a dull world turn to white
Then ghosting dim turn into night
A light went on inside the house
Flooding the pane with warmth to share
And lit the snow a golden square

SUMMER RAINDROPS

Let us take to the people joy
Put a dark accent on the tree
On to the roof a dancing toy
On to the sidewalk drop some glee

Let us add to our rain some charm
Cast down our raindrops soft and warm
Show the world we mean it no harm
Let us make it a happy storm

SUNSET

From sinking sun
Deep shadows run
Into the night
The dim slopes fail
As crests regale
Themselves with light

The canyon walls
Sheer waterfalls
Beseech the sky
The dusk grays rock
A silent clock
Says day must die

BLUESTEM GRASS

I stood alone, in the prairie,
A mote of dust so small was I
Inside the space of its vastness
That fringed along an endless sky

The sweep of long grass, from its past,
Was calling out across the main
Longing whispers to those before
That tracked its earth by wagon train

I wondered if along the hills
They might have stood here at this pass
Wondered if they felt humbled too
When they saw God's vast bluestem grass

AN OLD-TIME AUGUST

When the sun fills up the sky with brass
And the air is like a furnace blast
When the old boardwalk is blazing hot
The housewife pulls down the curtains taut

When your hope is that the rains come soon
When you step outside a darkened room
Where the sunlight glare hits like a fist
And you squint your eyes for something missed

When the dust is like a burning torch
And barefoot boys race to a porch
When the fields lie burnt before the town
August has put on its old-time gown

Sunset on the sea near Ixtapa, Mexico.

SUNSET ON THE SEA

There on the seashore upside down
Lie tons of ragged rocks
Across the ocean streams a path
Of silver shining locks

Along the west the purple tide
Shows strips of scarlet bar
Along the boundless water deep
The sky and ocean spar

The golden tresses of the sun
Give in to night and die
They go like blossoms to a grave
Out where the galleons lie

ICY VISIT

Icy made a visit last night
Enveloped in a mask of fog
He laid down crystal everywhere
And left the morning icy bright

The only dark was sheathed with glaze
Like trunks of trees and fingered limbs
That looked out through a glassy sheet
On death and dreams and frosty haze

WINTER LIGHT

There is an eerie winter light
Foreboding in its might
That takes its shape late afternoon
And filters crystals in the cold
That puts the world on silent hold
The winds will not impugn

Out in the western hills' white palm
The sun sets ghostly calm
Slanting a misty light to snow
It glazes pink one last remark
That yields to the advance of dark
And glooms a frosty glow

WINTER SNOWSTORM

The day brought snow, was fence-post deep
The sky was low and held in gray
Beneath the snow and comatose
The flowers slept and dreamed of May

The only warmth was near the stove
The other rooms were sharp with cold
And in the night the north winds came
That brought more snow for drifts to fold

The storm was nature with its fangs
And when the winds shook house and door
It blew with sounds of stalking death
That raced across the hardwood floor

Through wood the cold crept through the house
Through cracks it pushed its wild complaint
All fraught with doom and deep despair
The wind moaned on without restraint

I heard its sharp and cutting cries
Its murmur and howling of pain
Out in the woods, out by the barn
And coming down the snow-filled lane

In the morning the storm was gone
It left the world all buried in snow
Left a silence beneath the sky
Where nothing stirred but light and glow

The Flint Hills south of Manhattan, Kansas.

WINTER SNOW

Down comes the winter snow
A slanting in a blow
And dims the world

The northern gusting wind
Into a dither bends
And drifts a bed

The ice shuts waters deep
Where both lie sound asleep
In the grim cold

The lonely trees fringe stark
With a white dusted bark
Along the sky

BY THE LAKE

By the lake, works a snake
Between the shore and road
Dark eyes glued on his food
An unsuspecting toad

Careless there, pumping air
The snake strikes out en masse
Unleashes coil from the soil
And from the bluestem grass

TALES OF AFTERNOON

I feel the wind upon my cheek
Like kisses sent from far away
I watch the filtered sunlight gleam
Together with the shade of day

Along the webs of darkened limbs
I hear the leaves to others tell
Endearing tales of afternoon
That hold me in their captive spell

EACH COULD BURY ME

The sea comes in and curls
Upon itself unfurls
Comes from a boundless store
Over the bedding pearls
And breaks a shore in swirls

The sounding is a roar
The waters rush to shore
The sea with its demand
Takes what it can to floor
And leaves the rest to pour

The shore is backed by land
The sea by Neptune's hand
Is it by land or sea
The sea in rock has panned
And left behind the sand

Where would I like to be
To be with land or sea
I think the land is grand
But then, so is the sea
And each could bury me

SUNSET TALK

Why all the rush for night to come
Why must I go and end my day
The setting sun to this expounds
And gives the clouds a pink bouquet

The sunlight dims and puts on dusk
That turns the brush to gray down low
Behind the hills all tucked in bed
The sun consents to afterglow

It quickly brushes red and gold
Along the hills of fading light
The twilight trees are shading black
When to the sunlight speaks the night

You had your share of morning sun
You had your share of afternoon
Now comes the part of day I share
That excites the man in the moon

WINTER

Nature is at its winter
The day is afternoon
The wind is blowing bitter
Against the house a tune

The world is under blanket
The tree is draped with snow
The hills are void of racket
Crystals are in the glow

THE SPIDER AND THE MOTH

I saw a spider rappel a rope
Between the house and birch tree limb
His skill at webbing bears more than hope
It snares a moth within its net

I saw him pounce on its paper wing
Encompass it with hairy sting
If balance can be so small a thing
If life can hang by such a thread
Then we should very cautious tread
All through the days and nights to bed

REDBIRD

A redbird sat upon a limb
He looked me in the eye
He leaned far out upon his stem
And made as if to fly

Instead he thought it best to sing
He stretched and blew his trill
Until the air was filled with ring
He flew, and now it's still

WILDFLOWERS

I saw some wildflowers parade
In a grass meadow by a lake
They greeted me with a bloom's smile
Worked by the winds they bent and swayed
"Come be with us and stay awhile"

The vulnerable blossoms cried
Yet deaf, I picked them from the earth
Then wondered why for Heaven's sake
And how I suffered when they died
When I looked down at my mistake

TIMBERLINE

I walked up through the gnarled pine,
Where winds raced cold, and life severe,
Through weathered rock and close to fear
Along the trails at timberline

I walked below a sky-bridged pier
Of upthrust rock, frozen and high
Like a sleeping giant in the sky
The lifeless scene was bleak and sheer

I turned my thoughts from mountains high
And wandered down a pine-clad slope
Through flowered grass and aspen hope
That life renewed will never die

A SUMMER GONE

The sumac is turning
The meadows yearning
For a summer gone

Through pods that rattle
The long winds prattle
With the dying leaves

A lonely autumn sun
Paints hues finely done
On the silent trees

Out of the green behold
Comes brown, red, and gold
Whispering of home

CEDAR AND OAK

From out of the hills a dreaming
The grasses were in a green cloak
The slopes were soundlessly harking
To the sounds of cedar and oak

In the trees the birds were singing
Their shadows flitting like fairies
On acorns sunlight was gleaming
On cedars it frosted the berries

STANDING IN THE SURF

I standing in the surf alone
Feel the waves rush past to shore
Feel the purple seaweed thrown
Feel the sand drifting on its floor

I feel the mist of water blown
Feel the water round me pour
Feel the stir of deep unknown
Feel a force from the ocean's core

THE BEE

I hear the roar of a speeding car
That is the buzzing bee
Racing by in stripes of gold
From flowers to a tree

His industry is honey
To reimburse the store
Watch closely, don't let him sting
Or hear one hundred roar

He races from the hive to flower
He hums upon the nest
He crawls around the blossoms
On fingers without rest

When you go about the day
Do not on him intrude
The sovereignty of his work
Can make him very rude

WINTER WHEAT

The winter undressed the hillside
Froze up the summer seep
It put to bed the wildflower
Without the slightest peep

The winds are working the bluestem
Beneath a crystal sky
Skirting the hills are cedar trees
Their bending limbs awry

A river runs along the hill
Fringing ice at the sand
Across the silent bottom soil
The wheat is making stand

Beside the barren landscape
The wheat shines summer sheen
But yet I know it wants the snow
And ermine on its green

EVENING

The evening is painting a sunset
The night is shading down
The clouds are glowing rosette
The hills wear gold for a crown

From out of the dim the whippoorwills sing
Dark shapes are looming high
Low in the brush small noises ring
Trees silhouette in the sky

The landscape is turning from green to black
Winds are blowing a breeze
The moonlight gleams a streaming track
Through housetops, meadows, and trees

THE FOUR SEASONS

What happened to the springtime?
Where did the summer go?
The birds flew in, then out with fall
And winter brought its snow

As often as the woods green
As often they turn brown
As often as the hills undress
They put back on a gown

Nature forgot to tell me
Just where each season lies
Where do they wait out there in space?
Where in the arching skies?

IVY

An ivy blankets
A cottage wall
It clings to the stone
With leafy shawl
Throws little shadows
Along its run
Beseeches the sky
Beneath the sun

A wind through the leaves
Rustles the green
Below the cornice
Spreads a cool screen
Fingering a crack
Or joint close by
Building a leafed fan
Toward the sky

WHAT I LIKE

It's always blacker before the dawn
I like the predawn black
To change and bring some color on
Let night know dawn is back

I like the gold in an autumn noon
The red in an ember spark
I like the spring and a full moon
While shadows gather dark

I like the flash of a falling star
Arching down a starlit sky
I like the wind that travels far
To pass and kiss goodbye

I SEE BEGINNINGS

The rainstorm broke before the dawn
The day came with a golden glow
Upon the wet storm-beaten hills
And on the trees of flats below

Along the shouldered limestone rims
Grown out of oceans turned to earth
I see beginnings, from the sea,
And from its ledges see its birth

FOSSILS

The sun shone on a new sloped cut
Sliced deep by dozers through a hill,
It left the bygone years exposed,
Of rock and shale that made a fill

Millenniums gleamed from the slope
The strata's fossils left imprints,
When they were buried, skin and bone
Had stamped the limestone like blueprints

RAINSTORM

Large looming clouds raced adrift
Beneath the blue of anxious skies
Along the faint and ghostly hills
The clouds were rolling darker eyes

Where lightning was playing games
Of hide-and-seek and touch-and-go
Illuminating the distance
Like guttered candles in a blow

Thunder boomed in the light-flared clouds
Like a cannon's burst of flanking fire
The wind and rain were lashing trees
With a thrust of frontal ire

The marching rain closed off the hills
The sky turned sullen as can be
Rain poured and roared from wind-tossed clouds
Like I was in an angry sea

WILD SOUTHWESTER

A wild and windy southwester
Came by and shook the door
The frantic wind all through the night
Complained along the shore

The wind called up an accomplice,
The clouds, to bring the rain
And it complied with raindrops thrown
Against the windowpane

The gusting wind took trees in hand
And tossed them to and fro
And if they tried to straighten up
Then it would fiercer blow

WINTER HILLS

In the hills alone
I hear winds moan
Hear roses weep

The frost winks an eye
Along the sky
Where summers sleep

On the twilight snow
Blue shadows grow
Where all sounds freeze

The filtered light ebbs
On limbs of webs
In leafless trees

Kansas River downstream of viaduct, Manhattan, Kansas.

WHAT I WANT

I want a shady nook
Beside a running brook
In more than memory

I want a purple mountain
Water spring for fountain
Where the tall timbers be

I want the swelling sea
To splash and spray on me
From the blossoming deep

I want the broken hills
The sounds of leaves and trills
To be there when I sleep

I want the morning sun
The sailing clouds to run
Across a brilliant sky

I want a soft warm wind
Peach trees to always send
Blossoms where I will lie

COOL SHADE

In the summer air
The tree could sense
I loved it there
Beneath its cool shade

It cast down a leaf
To brush my cheek
And bear my grief
Sacrificed, to ground

More leaves lent their art
By rustling music
It touched my heart
Like love from afar

THE RIFFLE

Riffle water fingers a strum
It sings in sands a longing hum
Splashing rocks in a steady drum
Probing nooks where crawdads come

Flowing past isles in a sashay
Musical time, musical sway
Sweeping along in every way
Swishing around the snags at bay

Searching, falling, in a tinkle
Little fall a mini sprinkle
Rushing on to fast unwrinkle
Running through a sunlight twinkle

It stays along the shore to chum
It stuns the minnow almost numb
To catch the thrashing of a crumb
To hear the ever-chuckling thrum

It flashes bright in silver gray
And it never stops in its play
Racing in vigor night and day
Into a pool's deep blue bouquet

FIERCE STORM

The colonel's storm looked bleak and grim
There came a calm in spite of him
Sent back to where all fierce storms go
Reshaping for another blow

The storm charged back with grim desire
More troops and artillery fire
Fierce blasting winds took land and tree
Wreaking havoc and whirling debris

WILD VIOLETS

I walked the hills near stream and woods
Umbrellaed with the sky
The grass and flowers where I looked
Enchanted my vast eye

Two violets were smiling there
By themselves in the sun
The other day I felt a frown
When I saw only one

AUTUMN PRAIRIE

From out of the summer so green
An autumn gold is seen
In all of its glory

From out of the endless prairie
The winds blast contrary
With another story

From out of the last wilting brown
Come shades of pinkness down
Coloring slopes of grass

From out of the evening far
There blinks an early star
Now bringing in the class

I WALK THE HILLS

In spring, in the bluestem, alone
I walk the hills, the dogwood brake
Along the ridges of weathered stone
Up where the long winds moan

I'm up beyond a purple lake
I'm where the land and sky divide
Behind me strings a path I make
Of bending grass left in a wake

I'm where the copse and grass reside
A place I like to call my own
I send my skill out far and wide
To find where mushrooms hide

SEASHORE

I like the sand, the mystic shore
The rotting hulk, the buried lore
The fringe where water races thin
The wave that rushes in again

I like the sound of ocean's roar
The spray of water, salt, and spore
The walk from asphalt car-parked lot
Through soft white sand the sun left hot

Where tufts of grass like tawny hair
Display from sand dunes here and there
But I like more the slope to sea
That makes a place for you and me

MORNING

When sunrise approaches the hour
And night is thinking day
When we can see the turn in space
Before we see the gray

Predawn is a message springing
The birds will somehow hear
And it stirs their throats to singing
With daylight coming near

The eastern hills are brighter now
And lights the distance clear
The golden ribbon on the hill
Becomes a fiery sphere

The sunlight shines out in amber
And runs from tree to tree
The hills take off their purple coats
In sudden alchemy

The sun is blazing glory
Above the hilltop rims
The fleeing shadows hide away
In cracks and under limbs

The sun arches across the sky
A bird of fire awing
To measure off another day
To arc another ring

It soars aloft to deeper sky
No greater height is won
Than where sun sails the morning by
On its ancestral run

THE RIVER MUSHROOM

In the spring, in the woods alone
Where coyotes run and bury bone
Where the sand runs without a stone
Where the violets like to bloom
I looked in brush and fallen leaf
On sloping banks, for golden throne
The wily lodging held so brief
By that tasty king, the mushroom

MOUNTAIN TALK

Up high along a flashing stream
Where God and Angels come to dream
Where mustangs trail a mountain pass
I wander through the sego lilies
Like stars in a meadow of grass

I track slopes of aspen and pine
The needle straw, and columbine
Shadows gather at age-old rock
Under the trees, below the rim
And join the moss in mountain talk

THE BEE AND I CAN SHARE

I have a love that flourishes
In the depths of my heart
Where flowers bloom in meadows
Where bees are at their art

To the bee life is a flower
And pure country air
To him it all is ecstasy
The flower his lone affair

His desire is for the blooms
Where he is a welcome guest
There working with busy fingers
He hunts around the nest

That's the love that's in my heart
Flowers and country air
It gives me a peaceful feeling
The bee and I can share

LEAVES OF AUTUMN

The day was gray and overcast
Autumn was beauty at its last
The sky was low, the ground was stone
The air was chilling to the bone

I walked a path filled up with leaves
Beneath the barren limbs of trees
Where yesterday the limbs were plush
A freeze put leaves down in a rush

Before me laid the leaves out neat
No human being could repeat
Could leaves left stirred be a mistake
Where now there troughs a man-made wake

SHADES OF GREEN

The grassy throne
Of hilltops moan
Before the wind

The oak and cedar
Together spar
Along the slope

The firs twinkle
Leaves unwrinkle
In shades of green

If not by theme
The shadows scheme
Out of the sun

COUNTRY SNOWSTORM

The sky filled up with overcast
As far as eyes could see
It permeated the landscape
That stuck to ground and tree

It ghosted the trees and houses
In misty clouds and low
That drifts the far-off landscape
Behind a sky of snow

It sent the chickens to their roosts
The horses to the shed
The beaten dusted dog to porch
The cat to house and bed

THUNDERSTORM

Out of pouring rain
From across the main
And distant hills

The thunder muttered
Then boomed and rumbled
In closer spills

Intermittently
The dark canopy
Of clouds was lit

As lightning flashed
And the thunder crashed
The night was split

COLD TWILIGHT WALK

I wandered out and touched the gold
Of looming twilight shading cold
I pushed through sheets of blowing snow
Beneath a ghost of clouds aglow

The snow adhered and then would speak
To every footstep with a squeak
I like a shadow in the night
Walked in a cave of moving white

I then went back on altered ground
Beneath the wind and sweeping sound
And I felt death where it might roam
Until I saw the lights from home

THE DEEP WOODS

The deep woods stirred without a sound
The sunlight on the earth had hurled
Flecks on a pool where tree buds swirled
And bluegill dart through the water round
And ripple rings on mirrored glass
I stood there, solemn, in the grass
That came past knees in lush abound

The wind in whispers softly blew
A deer listened and then it fled
A squirrel raced to trees ahead
And further on a pheasant flew
Did this excitement in the air
Stir me on till I found the snare
And freed the rabbit caught in the slough

THE SNAKE

Slither slither in the grass
In the fringes of the brake
What walking mortal next will pass?
Disturbing coiled-up mass

Who would dare touch a hissing snake?
What feet would go too close with sense?
What else can make the body quake
Or freeze you cold when it's awake

What makes the terror so immense?
What grand deed can it profess?
I've never seen it but intense
Or but keep me in suspense

I never once, I must confess
In the grass, or brake as guest
But what its whiplash, strike, and press
Will pierce my bones with fright and stress

MOUNTAIN VIEW

Way up high the mountain winds cried
Beneath the steep where rocks collide
I wandered through long slopes of pine
Through tufted grass and columbine

I stood in awe of mountains' sweep
The drop to deserts purple deep
The sinking sun flamed on the rim
Above the canyons dark and dim

Then flames renewed in the dying glow
As if the sun chose not to go
I watched the shadows sweep the fire
And then I saw the rim retire

SEPTEMBER CATERPILLARS

As far as I could see
Caterpillars were crossing
The long blacktop road
Hundreds of them from the fields

The ranks of furred round bodies
Were swaying in waves
Like the prairie grass
Bending before the winds

They crept every direction
But each in a straight line
Went somewhere in a hurry
Where? almost as if it knew

THE OWL

There
On a white limb
In a large cottonwood
Sat a gray and wise old owl
He blinked lids on moonstruck eyes
With a stern surmise
He necked around
His hunting ground

Out
Of the vast dim
He hooted to the moon
To his mate or startled prey
Then soared into the nighttime hue
Of the fearful slough
For a quick blur
Or little stir

Wise
No not really
Just eyes that meet his needs
Those big old eyes like glasses
Are used for nocturnal hunting
The day too blinding
For those round eyes
We think look wise

SANDY SEASHORE

Each wave drifts in a bit of sand
Each back wave pans more sand to land
And builds a strip of pristine strand

Take the seashore from its first day
Must favor sand to that of clay
And more than seas can ever lay

Enough of sand to build a shore
Enough for dunes to bury more
Enough for waves, a place, to pour

DAWN

    Night is trembling
    Day assembling
    An empty space

    Dawn's gray finger
    Cannot linger
    Or slow sun's pace

    Red ribbons flare
    On golded hair
    And shining face

Between Ouray and Silverton, Colorado.

CALLING

I hear the vast desert calling
Out of the boundless unknown
Out of the silent distance
Of cactus, sand, and stone

I hear the soft trade winds urging
In sounds of the Coral Islands
Where surfs send sky blue waters
Rushing across the sands

I hear the far mountains singing
Across a gray-green prairie
And no voice in Heaven or Earth
Can match this song for me

RIVER FLAT COTTONWOODS

I ride along an oak-clad hill
To the east are the river flats
Of wild grass, fields of lush crops
And vast acres of sandy soil

In the distance the cottonwoods
Like a painting of feathered plumes
Chain along the river in walls
And patches of various heights

Down the road is just such a patch
In their shade I stop to listen
To the leaves rustle in the winds
Mimicking the sounds of water

THE AUTUMN COTTONWOOD

A low harvest moon
Rose above the hill
Tree leaves were gleaming
In the moonlight spill

The leaves were dancing
In costumes of gold
And whispered secrets
Shamelessly bold

SUNLIGHT

Out in the woods I walked on leaves
Where sunlight flashed down through the trees
Sunlight dappled the tawny ground
In little flecks that danced around

Through wind-turned leaves into the shade
The light came down on brush and played
It whirled around in pirouettes
Beneath the flash of silhouettes

Cliff dwellings at Manitou, Colorado Springs, Colorado.

THE EMPTY LAND

Up in a high desert mountain
I watched a steel gray curtain
Of rain walking the peaks and sky
Driven by winds that blew it by

Standing there on a pine-clad slope
My thoughts were spruce and aspen hope
I heard the winds through branches sing
And looked at flowers near a spring

I walked on old unbroken ground
Out to a rim and splendor found
I thrilled to stand in empty land
Of upthrust rock and distant sand

RAINDROP

One little raindrop fell from the day
More drops fell and gathered where it lay
Together they raced down a street

Where others joined to sweep it along
Into a pipe they thrashed into song
With a roar where darkness meets

It went from the pipe into a brook
Raced at the riffle, lounged at the nook
Out past the sight of sheltered men

Then God's hand took it to a cloud
Stored it away in a misty shroud
Until a want of rain again

THE SQUIRRELS

Out in the hills, south of the house
In a valley of trees and grass
Stood a group of old giant oaks
On a slight slope beneath a pass

I took Dad's .22 rifle
And walked through the oak-shaded light
With thoughts of shooting squirrels
But not a squirrel was in sight

It was like an empty schoolhouse
No sight of kids, or where they were
So I sat down on some old leaves
Then the squirrels began to stir

They raced on, behind, around limbs
Up and down trunks, swishing the leaves
Soaring in trees like high flyers
Bending limbs, in a summer breeze

I watched, then shouldered my rifle
Without firing a single shot
I marched back home, pleased as a bee
Within, without a painful thought

Dad asked me where my squirrels were
I told him they were on the hill,
And I did not want to disturb them
He said, "Maybe it was God's will"

SHADES OF NIGHT

Along the sky in shades of night
A star came down and hung a light
Between two streaming clouds of white
That drifted off like phony fears
The way a comet disappears

Light ghosts upon the cringing dark
On shadowed shapes where starlights park
Where trees loom up and, high, fringed stark
Where limbs and leaves, along gray skies lift
Down low were shadows, black, adrift

SWISS ALPS

The sheer mountains steep
Rise up to the sky
There is no season
The snow will die

On the slopes beneath
Winter snow and ice
Comes the alpine green
And edelweiss

REDBIRD AND BABIES

May, the backyard in a hue bush
A redbird nest two feet from ground
With four speckled miniature eggs
The mother flew to any sound

And I did my best to not disturb
In several days there was a birth
A helpless little primeval
Lay in the nest and new to Earth

Today the nest and birds were gone
The nest aground and torn apart
Scattered feathers glared on the ground
And I was with a heavy heart

A question wrinkled on my brow
How could Nature be so cruel
I think there should be some new law
Exempting redbirds with this rule

Broadmoor Lake, Colorado Springs, Colorado.

NATURE TALK

The winds of Heaven sing forever
The riffles thrum upon a drum
Sea waves crash and work their lever
The honey bees in cadence hum

The willows tell a rustling tale
The redbirds whistle Nature's talk
The snakes are hissing, lashing tail
The deer are soundless in their walk

The butterflies fly speechless words
The crows send word out in a call
Coyotes yell to the flying birds
The frogs go public with their gall

The thunder scolds without a choice
The crickets squeak their violin
The raindrops hit and then rejoice
The silent sun ticks on within

APRIL

The newborn leaves are shining
The wind is softly stirring
The birds are all a'chirping
April is on the go

Last night the clouds were weeping
Today the vines are creeping
The blooms are done with sleeping
Beneath the winter snow

The grass is green and gleaming
The sun is nearer warming
The far-off woods are calling
Morels begin to grow

TWO BAKER'S DOZEN

Two baker's dozen birds they were
The chickadees were making a stir
Helter-skelter on limbs they mouse
In a thornbush north of the house

The bush lay hidden in the snow
Dark, thin limbs were a tangled net
Where birds hunkered, and wings flashed bright
That shook down snow to my delight

COLD WINTER WOODS

Outside, in winter woods, alone
Comatose trees slept in the bone
I left my footprints in the snow
As far on back as eyes could go

Beside me walked an eerie light
Silent and gray it closed in tight
It came through woods and drifted gloom
My God! I thought, I walked with doom

WARM SPRING MORNING

I was outside
Early in the morning
In the late spring of the year
When all the world was green

The air was calm
There was no other sound
But a whisper in the leaves
And the call of Nature's friends

I looked out far
Into distant silence
And watched the dawn paint a glow
On the hills and treetops

I watched shadows
Dance on long shaky legs
And then I was struck with awe
And a warm strange feeling

I stood in rays
Of the dawn's golden light
And felt the sun on me alone
On me, on no one else

TREES FRINGE BRIGHT

In the day's shadowed depths
Of shores along the sky
As the sun sank behind
The western hills to die

For a moment then gone
Trees fringed along a gold light
In bright hieroglyphics
That only God could write

FIRST FROST

The frost went by a lonely flower
The freeze froze down its head
And with a sweeping frosty scythe
Frightened the trees' leaves red

The piercing air of early frost
Coated the landscape white
It brittled stiff the morning grass
That glittered in the light

WHERE PIGEONS HOME

I rode my bike where pigeons home
I watched their proud parade
Their twaddled strut and dragging tail
The barn was old of wood and tin
The loft was open at each end
Where through hinged doors the pigeons sailed

Barn roof sections were eared and loose
Where pigeons marched its slope
And leaned about on spreading wings
Part of them flew and swung around
Then fluttered down, back on the roof
They shook feathers and turned to preen

AUTUMN HUE

The trees delicately laced
Like hand-stitched border, traced
Along a breathless sky

The leaves using colors bold
Were knitting yarns of gold
With shades of reds and rusts

From out of the autumn hue
Before a sky of blue
A seamstress was at work

NO MERCY

Far out in the desert
Half buried in the sand
Lay a chain of mountains
Within a barren land

A sky of sun above
And mounds of sand below
From a land of ashes
The winds of hot sands blow

The far distance shimmers
The drifting purple slope
Beyond the blue mirage
There springs no watered hope

The cactus blossoms glow
In the desert's beauty
Belying the desert
That has no mercy

BLACKBIRDS

A haze of gray drifted the day
A day when leaves and acorns fall
Outside I heard a crowd of chatter
Beside the porch I heard them call

Blackbirds overflowed our large oak
They pushed and shoved on limbs to perch
I heard a distant shotgun blast
That brought in more to pew and church

They settled down to making noise
So skittish, their stay was in doubt
More fluttered in and shoved the next
Their noise of wing sent others out

A screen door slammed and sent them off
Any sharp sound would have done the same
In unison they exploded
To startled flight like coveyed quail

Peace then settled on the oak tree
A lone bird left behind then chirped
Startled at the silence it flew
To a distant tree of dim chatter

ROSE BOUQUET

The darkness outside was racing
The trees were lighter high
Large dark shapes were looming beneath
White diamonds in the sky

From out of the eastern horizon
The dawn was painting tan
When all of a sudden daylight
Spread open like a fan

Then came the bursting pods of flowers
In blooms of rose bouquet
That changed the night from shadowed black
Into the hues of day

Season's first snow.

A COUNTRY FREEZE

The sky was low and gray
The air felt damp all day
And pierced the skin with cold

The twilight painted dim
Along the distant rim
Then disappeared with night

The night came on with mists
Along the woods in drifts
That ghosted looming trees

The night brought in the cold
And laid the leaves down gold
Around the bared tree's feet

At dawn the barn glowed bright
Its roof a frosty white
The barnyard was ravaged

The cows' hooves small and round
Had churned up all the ground
And it had frozen that way

EARLY MORNING

Out in the morning on a hill
And when the land was sleeping still
The city lights were brightly on
And then went out before the dawn

Nothing in life I might have missed
Could be more grand than light through mist
The shading off of blackest night
Outside the glow of dawning light

I saw white clouds mixed with silver
Strung out endless on the river
And in the brakes there passed a gale
Of light that raced a gleaming sail

THE PLUSH GREEN FOREST

Deep inside the plush green forest
There is an amethyst pool
The leaves on trees are emeralds
That dangle, still and cool

The forest is a room of gems
Dead wood and leaves are floor
The walls and roof are leaves and limbs
Brush hang emeralds more

In this green room shy flowers bloom
For girls, pink brooches wait
While riffles show wet diamonds
Inside the green estate

SATURDAY MORNING SUN

At break of dawn when all asleep
I saw the sun peek through the deep
I saw her foot on a ladder steep

I saw her through the mist of day
I saw the bronze from out of gray
Then firm her grip the right to stay

I saw her linger for awhile
And then she went an extra mile
As I went fishing with her smile

MOON OVER MANHATTAN

I looked out through my windowpane
Into the night and black of space
In the sky a silver dollar
Over Manhattan gleams with grace

The moon encased in velvet sky
Inlaid with diamonds on its gown
Hypnotized the mosaic glitter
Of jeweled lights across the town

RISING SUN

I stood there on the wharf alone
Thinking back on the days I've known
I stood beneath a harbor light
Inside the mist of ghosting night

It was the time before the dawn
When dewdrops necklace on the lawn
I saw or thought I saw someone
That walked into the rising sun

The dim figure rose in the glow
And disappeared in mist like snow
I looked but could not find the gent
And wondered where on earth he went

A BUTTERFLY

I was mind-deep in selfish grief
In the grasp of its might
I could see no sign of relief
Save that the day was bright

I looked outside through my window
I saw the monarch fly
It shifted from high to low
And looked me in the eye

It tried the glass pane to alight
And staggered like a toy
It swung around till out of sight
And broke my day with joy

SNOWFLAKES

From the sky came busy snowflakes
And coated dim the creek and brakes
They filled the sky, covered the ground
Clung fast to brush and trees around

Upon creek water flakes adhered
Slowly melted and disappeared
The snowflakes changed the shore to white
And fringed the flow with icy light

The snowflakes molded into shapes
And built up drifts and hanging drapes
Some took to winds in bitter flights
To swirl at roofs and outside lights

DAY

I like to see a lemon dawn
Bursting out in rose bouquet
As all the leaves keep tune
I like the shade upon a lawn
The light to change from zenith day
To hues of afternoon

I like to see the sunlight bend
From gold to pink in afterglow
Along an evening sky
I'd like a soft caressing wind
Out where the apple blossoms blow
To be there when I die

SPRING

The blossoms, the bee
Love a tree
On springtime day

The sun, the moon
Play a tune
In their own way

The rain, the dawn
Tease the lawn
When it is May

INTO THE DEEP

I looked into
The heart of night
I saw the stars
Glow dim and bright

I felt a sense
Of distance leap
As I looked out
Into the deep

FIRST LIGHT

From out of darkness comes the day
It grays the black from rim to rim
And ghosts the trees across the way
Where woods are looming through the dim

The paling stars are blinking out
A hoot owl soars to tree and bed
A rooster crows and with his shout
Announces morning to his shed

THE WAY IT IS

The ocean waves push
And push on the land
If not by the sea
It buries in sand

The mountain peaks push
Up where the winds whine
If not thrusting rock
It thrusts up pine

And the people push
And part the ozone
Endangering the light
And killing our own

CASE WON

I will stop your rampant way
Said the calm pool to the riffle
Needing satisfaction for its grievance
The pool sought an injunction

It carried its case to court
Let the record show its verdict
The riffle must stop its vigorous ways
When it enters the plaintiff's pool

SUMMER DOWNPOUR

The rain drank up the dust
Then went its drunken way
Flashing, searching, finding
A path down to the bay

The clouds break up and run
The sun comes steamy hot
Then rests a golden finger
Upon the land in thought

Sea wave.

THE SEA WAVE

Sea water rolls into a swell
That leaves a trough behind
The swell becomes a racing wave
With shore deep on its mind

The sea wave breaks onto the sand
Its rushing starts a gull
The surfing water slowing down
Flows round a wooden hull

The water then in flowing back
Smooths sand along the shore
And then there comes another wave
To blossom with a roar

THE DESERT

From out of sun-scorched tortured land
From out of soundless desert sand
From out of cactus, out of dune
There comes to ears a mystic tune

Through arroyos and lava flows
Through blossomed noons and sun-streaked glows
The cholla jump, the soft winds groom
Dust devils whirl, wildflowers bloom

Beneath a barren mountain pass
In a sanctuary of grass
Through cat-claw and Indian thistle
Come sounds of wren and quail's whistle

Through creosote bush and mesquite
Through yucca plants and winds of heat
Through skies of bronze and cold dark nights
The old ones sing enchanted rites

A BRIGHT WINTER DAY

The sunlight was shining
Frost sparkled below
Where people were scooping
A path through the snow

The landscape was sleeping
Deep blanketed white
And my eyes were squinting
Against the glared light

The sparrows in cedars
Sent snow aground
Swept loose from the fir boughs
They feathered around

A sharp breeze was lifting
Fine snow in play
And dusted my clothing
A bright winter day

Mesa Verde, between Durango and Cortez, Colorado.

DEEP CANYON

I walked down a deep canyon of high sheer walls
Beside a stream and waterfalls
I heard the birds singing above the roar
As I went down its rock-strewn floor

Its high walls narrowed to the racing stream
Brush and willows and watered gleam
Then it widened out to a lovely glade
Of grass, pine, aspen, light and shade

Old trees on rims were soundlessly lifting
Gnarled fingers and arms beseeching
Where a vast stark solitude took my eye
To a bright blue ribbon of sky

SPRING SUNSET

The sinking sun
Shines on the rim
The mountain peaks
Grow golden trim

Below, the trees
Of green turn gray
The shadows race
Along the way

The twilight glooms
Beneath the glow
Then disappears
Like melting snow

HOW THE SUN AND MOON ROSE

Deep from a sleep the sun rose
Along the hills in growing glow
Before the hills could see their toes
The sun rose red as priestly robe
Then turned into a golden globe

Into the darkness the moon rose
Along the hills lit dim and gray
Before the night thought darker woes
The moon rose peach and then it fell
Into the paint of silver shell

Love

Near Rannells Road in Manhattan.

THANKSGIVING MORNING

I rose from bed before the dawn
The sky was dark and deep
Across the eastern hills and sky
I saw some color creep

I stood and watched the creeping light
The hill before the sun
Where raced a light on the hilltop
Like quail on the run

I, as the sun and hilltop touched
A moment in the day
Thought, did not the sun touch your eyes
The rain touch Earth in play

Did not the tears of grief or joy
Touch your warm heart and cheek
Did not the wind touch the treetops
And then through others seek

Did not the moonlight touch your hair
Touch the land and the sea
With all of Nature a'touching
Then why not you and me

THE FACADE

It was all
A facade
Her beauty
A fraud

Subterfuge
Hidden well
Broken words
That fell

Avarice
Lies to spurn
Where is love
I yearn

I SHALL REMEMBER

I shall remember when life becomes dim
The way you teased me with your eyes
How you made me feel like a man again
Then you left me with low gray skies
And memories that often arise

I shall remember your alluring smile
As life erodes down through the years
How I would see you in the wildflowers
Clad with the dew of morning's fears
Until the sunlight had dried the tears

I shall remember when I see moonlight
Go down my bedroom with a sweep
How you and the shadows would play with night
Though my heart's broken and I weep
I shall remember in thoughts and sleep

LEAVE ME SOMETHING

When they placed her there on the shelf
It felt right that they should
She came to me in porcelain
And I was wearing wood

I was deep in dust and lonely
In a room's silent ways
But when she came I heard the leaves
From out of long past days

I knew they would not leave her there
Someone of royalty
Would want to purchase her figure
I told her soundlessly

Leave me something for when we part
Something for my heart's sake
Leave me something like words of love
To keep me when awake

I HEARD SWEET MUSIC

I heard sweet music in the air
It blessed my ear and blessed my soul
The music came, I know not where
But I know love was singing there

It was music that heaves the heart
Swelling it like an ocean tide
A song of love that jolts a start
Rushing blood to a pounding heart

It was sweet music I heard play
Do not think me mad or tease me
I heard the tune, I sensed the sway
'Twas when I kissed your lips today

TOGETHER

Her lips were full and red
Her eyes were silver blue
My breath grew thin and fled
When I saw her anew

The dreary days were long
When we were far apart
Together I heard songs
That shouted in my heart

THE TWAIN SHALL MEET

The rain, the snow
I somehow know
Will always be
The tears run deep
Where heartstrings weep
Inside of me

The sun, the sky
In passing by
Relieve the smart
The twain shall meet
And always treat
A broken heart

FIRST MEETING

The complaining wind was blowing
Then stopped to be polite
It seemed to want to please me
With smaller puffs of might

It was a brassy sun that filled
A sky of afternoon
Sunlight dappled on the shadows
The leaves were keeping tune

I thought, there must be sundry tunes
That minds and heartstrings play
When life and love and couples come
Together their first day

I TOOK THE MOONLIGHT

Late last night I took the moonlight
With thoughts of love and thoughts of you
I put it in my mind's gold book
And wished that you could have it too

I took the moonlight's painted sheen
On me, and landscape, brushed in gray
Took in the silence in between
The heart of night and dawn of day

The light through trees flashed with a glow
And lit the shadows silver blue
Before the moonlight went away
I put it in this verse for you

THE DARKENED NIGHT TO DAY

From our first moment that we shared
I felt songs rise I had not sung
I had not felt that way since young
When life was wrapped in arms of joy
And it felt good to be a boy

Where did the years go in between
My youth, and now, no wasted left
I think for me life's biggest theft
You gave to me in one short hour
Another spring of blossomed flower

Maybe in life that is enough
You took my heart and made it sing
My ear within could hear the ring
You showed to me a better way
To fly from darkened night to day

PRETTY EYES

When you look at me with those black eyes
I see in them no shame
So don't look down but let them rise
Or are you at another game?

When those pretty eyes look down I fear
A trust you will betray
Why do I think they never tear
Why do you want me anyway?

How many others have you beheld
How many all alone
How many more have you expelled
What will you do when youth is gone?

HIDDEN LOVE

Your lingering touch upon my arm
Was it a transfer of your fire
Was it a touch of covert love
Asking for my desire

Are you secretly drawn to me
Did someone tell you what they heard
Could you have seen through my facade
Could you have discovered

A LIFE TO MAKE

Into the smoke and dusty light
Into the dimness of the room
She came, a friend out of the night
Into my heart of dismal doom

Out of the pain of distant fire
Out of the depths for beauty's sake
She lifted me with her desire
And gave to me a life to make

SHE WAS GONE

It was chance put us there
A stranger and her smile
And with our vibes we share
A little while

We had our things to do
And in the room we part
I did not know her name
Or where to start

I felt within a panic
As death began to dawn
I looked around the room
And she was gone

LOVE ME NOW

What good is love without honor
What good is love without liberty
What good is love if it be cruel
What good is love if you're not there
And if it hurts, can it be love

So if you love me, love me now
To love me now is only fair
So do not wait till I grow cold
Don't let me go unloved to Heaven
For one not certain, nor too bold

THE SUN ROSE

The clouds were stormy, the days dim
My heart was dead within
Today the sun rose in the sky
To shine on me again

I found this burst of happy joy
Coming from God and you
He resurrected my dead heart
You made it sing like new

IF I COULD BE A PRETTY FLOWER

If I could be a pretty flower
And if it was your will
You could place me on your breast
Or on the window sill

If I could be a cotton glove
You wear a bitter day
Then I would hold your hand
Till winter went away

If I could be a silken dress
I then to you would cling
And with every swinging step
Your garment's joy would sing

TOO RISKY

I thought it better
To have what we had
Than nothing at all
But she was not sure

I tried to soothe her
But she determined
Frightened as she was
I was too risky

So she turned inward
Closed doors were safer
Though inside, four walls
Were crushing her will

THE PURPOSE

We all need love
In our hearts
Or all else is hopeless

Everybody
needs someone
Or what is the purpose

NEAR BUT FAR

How near the dawn
But yet so far
So maybe that's
The way we are

The dawning light
Will kiss the reed
Maybe your kiss
Is all I need

PANIC

Can we kiss once
And kiss no more
Can we love once
Then shut love's door

Can we touch passing
Each other by night
Never touch again
Come again to sight

Would you panic
With just the thought
As it did me
If we were naught

I NEED YOU

To live I need you
Like I need the air
But when I breathe
You are not there

You are a mirage
Beckoning, but not
I feel the cold
But I am hot

I feel like the bee
That always needs more
Sweetened nectar
To sip and store

A NOTE IN THE WIND

I hear a whispering
In the southwest wind
That blows my yard a note
To a grassy end

From its journey afar
This thin note of blue
Just says "I am lonely"
With no other clue

Somewhere in the Southwest
Lives a kindred soul
We both are listening
For peace bells to toll

CUPID

I was busy in my den that day
And felt a little queer
As if someone were watching me
Quite close from somewhere near

Beheld by some enchanted eye
Then, there across the floor!
I saw the traitor peek around
A half-closed closet door

His startled look betrayed the shock
His little act was caught
He darted to the living room
Dove in a flower pot

Oh sakes, the thought of love in here
Called for his quick defeat
And my potted window foliage
Was not a safe retreat

The little scoundrel's fate was sealed
I'd flush him out and far
So I went to the kitchen nook
To fill a water jar

I went back in and drenched the elf
To make the cherub stir
It overflowed the flower pot
And drowned the little sir

I thought a burial the proper thing
For such a noble foe
But when I went to get him out
He stood there with his bow

Too late I saw the pointed shaft
I felt a tiny smart
The jubilant rascal's arrow
Had hit me in the heart

SENSUAL CURVES

When she was in the candlelight
My love awing would soar
My thirsty heart was drinking wine
When done it asked for more

Her clothes could not conceal her form
Nor lines of given grace
And when her eyes stole looks at me
My blood would always race

Each time I saw her sensual curves
My breathing breast went tight
And in my heart it felt like love
How, God, can that be right

VALENTINES

There is a knocking at my door
I look and see them run
Into the dawn like little stars
They race into the sun

The hearts are framed in golden glow
Bordered with rays of lace
They make a perfect valentine
But part without a trace

My thoughts are on the valentines
How you could have them too
And so I put them in this verse
A valentine for you

SOPHIA

She thought
She could hold me
Could enfold me
Like a mad housewife
Scold me

And so
Before she led
Me off to wed
Like a frightened cat
I fled

WE MET IN NATIONAL CITY

In the summer, in a park, in National City
I saw her black eyes looking at me
Through the longest lashes you ever did see
And her passionate red lips aglow

It was a night the stars shone soft and dainty
Like bedstraw flowers against the grass
We walked a carnival with people en masse
Before the bay and silver-strands sea

The Pacific trade winds gently teased her black hair
Like velvet against her creamy skin
Together just one night, I remember then
As though it were in yesterday's air

I often remember her when I'm lonely
If she would be as pretty today
I regret we never met again, in a way
But, to think of her brings love to me

FANTASY

When I watch you from a distance
Remote from me alone
Or when you come up close to me
My lips are heavy stone

You know me not, nor I know you
And love can never be
So let us only touch in dreams
And nights of fantasy

WITH SOMEONE

Maybe the dawn's light I love to see
Maybe the spring where blossoms be
Maybe the far mountain's purple hue
Maybe the sky when it is blue

Maybe the sea with its surfing roar
Maybe the woods and leafy floor
Maybe, but beauty lies just begun
Until I share it with someone

MOTHER'S LOVE

When I was young in days of old
Back there the golden sun patrolled
Cast sun and shade beneath the leaf
Days long before I knew of grief

My mother's voice broke into song
She held me close, secure, and strong
How deeply now that love I miss
Warmed in her breast and with a kiss

Spiritual

Family gathering.

HE ANSWERED MY PRAYER

I asked God for a house
I thanked Him every day
Riding by my empty lot
Until He said

"What about your faith
Without works it is dead
Shouldn't you go on and build"
And so I did

He answered my prayer
My feelings sang with song
Like when you're going home
And so I did

THROUGHOUT MY PASSING DAY

Memory of love sings to me
Out of the past it clings to me
It does the strangest things to me
Throughout my passing day

My God in Heaven will mold me
Take me in His arms and hold me
Like the distant hills enfold me
Throughout my passing day

A CATHEDRAL TUNE

I could hear an organ playing
From another street over trees
The people were singing
Some sort of cathedral tune
That rose up lonely in the breeze
Serenading a kindred moon

I wondered who the people were
Gathering to song so forlorn
No church was over there
Just rows of houses beaten low
Around the poor and the newborn
Planting God's word so it would grow

TIME'S STING

I watch the time
As it watches me
Without the benefit of eye
Or trembling at the knee

Yet, I tremble
As I watch the time
Patiently waiting, watching me
For no reason or crime

We must in time
Be in the real world
When we talk of this together
And unravel time's sting

WHAT'S REAL IN THE WORLD

Does anybody really love anybody
Or are all selfish
Selfish in varying degrees
Except for Jesus
Who is and remains selfless
Until the end of time
When is a friend really a friend
Surely after years of time
Or could it be only a day
When is time your time
Really your time, but you can't have time
For time has us
And like time, life is the same
For life has us
You can't even take your own life
It must take itself
Nothing seems to be anything
And anything seems
To really be nothing at all
Nothing's for long
For whatever is here is soon gone
Yesterday is gone
And what is here now is soon gone
Faster than you can speak
Faster than it can be written down
And what is to be
Is here only as long as it takes
Even a second
Can't be stopped before it's gone
And forever gone
And memories: Where do they stand
I mean really stand
Can you leave behind a mark

In this world
A mark to stand or is it unique
Like a shout in the dark
Forever lost in the space of time
Forever gone
Or when it is gone is it really gone
Except in memory
That may or may not return to us
As memories can
Why are we creatures of habit
In things we like
Except to bring back the moments
That cannot stay
And yet we strive on searching time
Our only hope
Is the hope of faith, the connection
That is for sure
Our only way out of this dream
That Adam put upon us
Our only reality in this life
And thank Heaven
We have the Bible to show us
The way is God and His word
The one thing that is real

CONJECTURE

I have conjectured about leaven
About the blood, about Heaven
Had thoughts and looked on Jesus there
I know the Bible, grace, and prayer

To comprehend is another thing
To know the touch, know the ring
Of death, like a sudden surprise
Opening the gates to Paradise

THE RAINBOW

I huddle in the cold wind
Around the cooling glow
Of the dying red embers
And dream of brighter fire

I cling tighter to my coat
Tighter to the rainbow
In my heart there is singing
To God and the Promise

UNTIL HEAVEN

I feel a need
For learning
To water the seed
In yearning

So I continue
At the Book
Dig and do
And look and look

To sustain me
until Heaven
And that dawn
Of conversation

NO COMPROMISE

Oh, the many compromises
In all of the things we do
If only Adam had not fallen
And life for all were true

Adam put God in a hard place
To save us and be true
I'm glad He did not compromise
In what He had to do

DOWN THE DEEP EARTH

If my blood should flow
On the concrete floor
Or down the deep earth
Let it in honor go

Obsessed with my God
In His lone bidding
Let my memories
Be fond beneath the sod

SUNDAY CHURCH

High in the steeple a swinging
All of the church bells are ringing
The steps are soundlessly greeting
The ushers are busy seating
The people are mutely waiting
With a facade of piety
It is the day of Sunday church

The choir down aisles is singing
The Priest is silently praying
The baby at mother is breasting
The communion plate is resting
The Priest is finally preaching
Out of the hour of deity
Out through the door the people lurch

THE BIBLE

The kings can have their riches
Give me the right to kneel
The generals can have their glory
Give me the Christian seal

The scholars can have their books
Give me the Book of all
Librarians' ears like silence
My ears hear prophets call

FIND EDEN

When the sun is burning embers
The sea and land divide
When the waves crash on empty shores
The winds race far to hide

It's time to go and leave it all
The night is growing late
Walk on past the fires to Eden
Walk in the garden gate

HE LET ME GO

But who
Might I ask that speaks to me in such woe
Would have me there abide
Identified
Without a throe

But how
Might I demur until the grasses grow
One more time there beside
Justified
With the rainbow

But why
I want again to see the blossoms blow
To see the ocean's tide
Satisfied
With the status quo

But where
Beyond the purple mountains' afterglow
And who will be my guide
Mystified
In what to trow

But when
That is what I want so much to know
When was it that I died
Crucified
He let me go

IS THERE STILL A PARADISE

Is there still a Paradise
Is there an upper room
Just out of reach of Satan
Beyond the fires of doom

Is it now an empty room
Since Jesus with the key
Opened the gates of Heaven
For believers like me

I know it is all conjecture
Faith is the way to go
But way down deep inside of me
I feel a need to know

GOD IS MERCIFUL

I spend the now as best I can
Let the memories work me well
My hope for you is just as kind
As kindness is . . .

I have walked the darkness of sin
Found it hard to face reality
At times in utter agony
But that is past . . .

I know what to do about sin
I know what it takes for Heaven
I know how faith comes, I know grace
It's in the Book . . .

I have asked God to forgive me
I always forgive those who ask
And God can't be less merciful
Than I am . . .

EACH NIGHT WILL DAWN

Each night will dawn into a day
How swiftly dawns fade into years
And then the years soon pass away
Into the race to death and tears

The coming days are shading down
How lonely sleep the creeping nights
Where darkness wears a wraith-like gown
Before far Heaven's distant lights

But dawn will always light the sky
How bright the dawns when life is best
And through death's door believers fly
To God non-stop in bright dawns west

DEATH

There was no sun up in the sky
No bluegill in the creek
No golden hue of afternoon
No warmth was on her cheek

No snow was on the mountaintop
No time for holding fast
It was almost like the Rapture
The now was in the past

Past all the tears of pain and joy
Beyond the last of fight
But what is that to a spirit?
On past the dark of night

The bay at Zihuatanejo, Mexico.

HEAVEN IS EVERYTHING

I have felt the sea upon my face
Faced the South Sea winds that blow
I have seen the sky in vastness race
And in the distant grass embrace
But yet in passing I see no trace

I have ridden boats on tides that glow
In the moonlight where moonbeams lie
I have drunk in streams that always flow
That taste of Rocky Mountain snow
And seen the shadows through canyons go

I have lounged in a back alley sty
Imbibing there in time and wine
I have lingered beneath a cloudy sky
Long in grief and agony's eye
More than once I have seen someone die

I have walked the trails in mountain pine
With ear to hear the aspen sing
I have watched the deer on grasses dine
Smelled the raindrops and dust combine
Seen views for God that are also mine

I have never heard a church bell ring
That saved a soul without God's grace
I have not seen an Angel on the wing
But I know Hell, I know its sting
And I know Heaven is everything

ODE TO RUTH

You came to me where the blossoms blow
Amongst the petals with a pretty smile
From out of the past with a sunlit glow
We were alone with God's word for a while
Then you went away from the hour we spent
Like a spirit without blemish or sin
You left me there with my dreams until dawn
From the roots of Moab your image was sent
That puts joy in my heart, to my chagrin
I looked everywhere but you were gone

You had disappeared like long-vanished years
I often remember my time with you
And long for something as the sunset nears
At times I have felt you close in the hue
Of an afternoon's shadow and sunlight
Along with the soft southern winds of day
The time of your leaving was just the start
Of the knowing that lights the dark of night
I was wrong when I thought you went away
For that time you left you went to my heart

CHRISTMAS 1979

I in the house on Christmas alone
The solitude pressed down like stone
The silence was like an eerie tune
And it depressed my afternoon

Memories came from my attic's mind
In that old dust of time I find
Past golden treasures, and in the gloom
I sensed something else in the room

Unable to quite grasp the sense itself
I saw my Bible on a shelf
My eager hands reached for what I've known
Blessed gift! I was not alone

THE UNBELIEVER

Oh ye of little faith
Wasting all your years
Your flesh is much too weak
To keep away the tears

You build up all your hopes
On the shifting sands
You speak in idle words
And wring your anxious hands

You yield to impatience
Listen to your peers
Stagger at the Promise
And bow your knee to fears

LISTEN TO MY HEART

I love and praise and worship You
With all my heart and soul
With all my spirit and being
And every church bell toll

I ask You, listen to my heart
And hear its pulses sing
With words I cannot now express
I send them off awing

To know You hear my heartfelt song
Stem winds me like a toy
That spins my spirit like a top
'Round and 'round with joy

THE TEMPLE OF GOD

I hear no native sound
Of surf or wind or crow
No sound as I now know
There is a calm stillness
Beyond sorrow and fear

Upon this hallowed ground
I hear no human word
Just a knowing unheard
Of some enchanted rite
That penetrates the soul

PASSION FALL

Bathsheba, primping, bathes
Reflections reveal her tools
Her fairest form, which weakens
An iron will that rules

David's will is not the first
Nor the last to passion fall
The first belongs to Adam
The last, hear Rapture's call

I WALKED THE WOODS

I walked the woods of silent trees
Upon a floor of last year's leaves
Where twilight shades all through the day
Where sunlight dapples, shadows sway

I walked in brush and prickly teeth
Through the tangles and weeds beneath
Smelled the air from recent showers
Scented with the earth and flowers

I walked by streams, through grassy vale
I asked myself where did I fail
I heard a whisper, "You failed not"
Thank God for grace, was what I thought

PRAYER

Give me the sunlight on my face
The wind's soft, warm embrace
Give me the sea and salty taste
The mountain's other side
Give me the sky, cloud-free and wide
The day too sweet to waste

Let me see all God's creatures preen
And see the woods serene
Let me wander the desert sand
Yet always be at home
Let me go where the Angels roam
Let Jesus sweep the land

THE WILL

On her shelf I found a Bible
Unused, God's will and testament
It was a gift from her parents
That she never opened

I wondered why it was not read
Maybe her lack of faith, a clue
I do know, she never enjoyed
Her vast inheritance

CHRISTMAS

This was the day
This was the morn
Jesus was born
So long ago.

He came for us
(Withstood the pain
Of Adam's stain)
And kept His word.

The son of God
Of virgin born
This joyous morn
So long ago.

YOUNG IN JESUS

Keep me, Jesus, from the cold
For I know you always care
Here I am exposed and bare
Keep me young and never old

As the eagle, renew my youth
Tell my Angel of what we share
My faith is strong, so is my prayer
I'm growing, Jesus, in the truth

WE MUST MOVE ON

To advance in life
Has no limits
Except those we set
Before our own path
By a lack of faith

So we must move on
To stop means death
What else can God do
But turn us to dust
When we are useless

QUESTIONS FOR MY ANGEL

Where is my fortitude
Where does the beauty lie
Where did all the days go
Seen by a dying eye.

What will God have to say
Where is the Grand Sire
Who will supply the love
That only I can fire.

Where is familiar look
Where is my boyhood town
Where is my bit of fame
My fragment of renown.

I KNOW

I know that I know
Who owns this land
Each piece of dirt
Each grain of sand

He lives far beyond
The mountain's rock
Out past the winds
Past need of clock

This land that I own
I will to seed
But still I know
Who holds the deed

A BOOK OF LIFE

My life is like the book
Unfinished yet to see
But Heaven when unveiled
Will make a place for me

So large is the mystery
It holds me in its spell
But life is there in Heaven
And death belongs to Hell

SPIRIT, SOUL, AND BODY

The spirit is the life alone
The soul can decide on its own
The body alone is dust or stone
And only two can see the throne

Together they make the world strong
Some say it's three, but they are wrong
The body goes where bones belong
And two will sing the crown a song

WEBS OF LOVE

A cloud diverges
The moon emerges
In the low sky

The shadows erode
Near a country road
Where moonbeams lie

The moonlight gleams bright
Filtering its light
With God above

The dim landscape stares
While the moonlight snares
With webs of love

TAKE ME

Take me where the roses blow
And seashores call
Past the grief I know
And tears that fall

Take me out to places far
That Angels keep
Past the gleaming star
And silence deep

Take me into tomorrow
Where all is light
Past the point of sorrow
And past the night

ZOE — LIFE

Deep in our hearts is Eden
The place we all desire
It holds the covert wisdom
To which we all aspire

Faith is the mighty power
Nearer than nearest room
For within its walls is Zoe
Without it is our doom

The Redeemer professes
It is the Christian aim
We find our way to Jesus
And there a life we claim

Oh, joy to Revelation
To look beyond the sea
To glory in the written word
And pierce Eternity

LOVE SONG FOR JESUS

You are like the music
That makes the body sway
You are like the lyrics
That take the breath away

You are like the Christmas
That fills the Christian air
You are like the snowflake
More pure than we, You bear

Is it any wonder
You saturate my sight
Why all else seems empty
And black and blank as night

GOD'S PEOPLE

Dark are the long winds
The fair winds part
Through the land and sea
God's people chart

Peace old hostile lands
Where long grass bends
God's people must ride
The western winds

Fair blow the long winds
Upon God's own
They hear His calling
To lands unknown

GOD HAS THE ANSWER

I suppose no one is ever
Happy with what they have
And the most important thing now in life
Has become difficult
So all your needs and your problems gall you
And they become an obsession

Become wraith-like and illusive
And always out of reach
Then you think your problem has no answer
For you this may be true
But for God it's not too difficult
Just ask Him and He will tell you

PAUL

Who is the greatest author of all
Whose words are time and never fall
Who can you name, men have read more
None on your list can equal Paul

Would you not say the greatest hand
Wrote words of truth to every land
Brought hope and faith and always love
And joy and courage to stand

Paul's words are life to every race
Remove death's Hell without a trace
Pour light to the New Testament
Paul, an old sinner saved by grace

GLORY

There can be no glory in war
To kill and maim is hate
The victor without forgiveness
Cannot pass Heaven's gate

We must be careful with glory
When there is only one
The God that resides in you
The Glory of the Son

FAITHFUL FAITH

I have been in deep travail
I have been in the deepest grief
Through it all I have kept the faith
And received my reward

I too have gone to God for help
On things I could handle myself
I know better, I have His grace
And that is sufficient

Garden of the Gods, Colorado Springs, Colorado.

TEMPORAL WORLD

Everyone must face what all face
There is no out, there is no grace
Ridicule not another's state
It may become your own fall fate

Everyone's time is time in all
And what things rise will sometime fall
Nothing's for long for time is change
That time in time will rearrange

FAITH

When I said that death was mine
To choose and pick the time to go
That was faith not ego
When I said without a throe
I believed it so

When God's Word said that the time
Was my measure and mine to claim
I claimed it in His name
And on the night that He came
I had picked the same

CHRISTMAS EVE AND MORNING

It was a snowy world outside
With brilliant stars above
It was the night of Christmas Eve
To celebrate God's love

The people on Christmas morning
To windows all looked out
They yearned for something out of sight
With eyes that searched about

I hope they found out there the gift
Not found in any mall
A prayer and praise to God would be
Sufficient for us all

THE OTHER SIDE

Out of the night the fair winds blew
Through all the days of what I knew
The winds came in through closed locked doors
And took me off to distant shores

I went through lights of something new
Placed near a lake deep icy blue
I could see the far high mountains
And at their feet gleamed grassy plains

I walked through flowers in the grass
The scent of blooms in flint hills pass
The rustling tree leaves, I could hear
With birds a'singing crisp and clear

I saw a home and large oak tree
My parents there awaiting me
I met old friends throughout the day
Not seen since they had passed away

Food was prepared for all to eat
Musicians played, to Heaven's beat
There was talk and laughter and joy
And I felt like a little boy

Then Jesus came aglow in light
And daylight bowed He shone so bright
He met me by the fish-filled pool
And briefed me on my starting school

GOD'S AGAPE

The secret to love is to give
Without the slightest shove
God's agape is overflowing
With everlasting love

No mountains nor the oceans deep
Can touch a distant star
No wind, nor snow, nor even rain
Can tell you where they are

But the heart can touch the Heavens
And give to you the key
It will tell you God's agape
Is blessed with charity

A LONGING QUEST

I have a longing quest
That I cannot touch
Nameless, just out of reach
But not by much

It may be something lost
From out of the past
Through the portals of time
Where no things last

It is something innate
A struggle in all
In a temporal world
From Adam's fall

It will end in Heaven
Where time is peace
Where joy is forever
And longings cease

AN HOUR AGO

I heard His call
A call I'd hoped some later date
He was about to leave me to sin
When He turned to shut the gate
But He let me in with no debate
Though I was a little late
An hour or so

He stood there tall
With a smile and merciful heart
And then we were together again
What seemed so long apart
And now again my life can start
Life that passed without a chart
An hour ago

JUDGMENT

What can one say of empty years
And what about those faithless tears
What about the times I knew no grace
What of the times I lost the race
I think He will understand.

What can I say about the truth
What of love, spurned, like that of Ruth
What of the faith I built on sand
What will God say when there I stand
I trust He loves me anyway.

GENTLE IN THE NIGHT

He came gentle in the night
And treated death as trite
No comfort did he offer me
Though anxious of the flight

Identified upon the scroll
I knew what was my role
I went gentle in the night
And never told a soul

TWO WORLDS

His Spirit shed a parting tear
And then looked back into the gloom
Yet this act of deathbed dying
Just meant that he was going home

He went as quiet as the night
Like light encroaches into dawn
His heart ran down and then two worlds,
An instant, touched and then moved on

My touch or voice could not bestir
His life in lands of seraphim
A cherubim must wake him up
For I cannot awaken him

PASSION BY ITSELF

Passion by itself
Has no bit or rein
No height, no width, no depth
Nor any brain

We all must struggle
With mind over matter
The will to dominate
Over the latter

For that reason, God
Said unto all men
"Obey my commandments
For peace within"

FLIGHT

I looked at an awesome vastness
Of empty space and clouds banked high
Purple and white cathedral doors
That arched across the sky

I looked at sun-streaked rays of light
Through stained-glass windows of the clouds
Light graced the airplane as it flew
Through walls of Heaven's shrouds

The space then blossomed out anew
Vast clouds around, above, below
And I caught a glimpse of Jesus
Surpliced and with a glow

I WILL NOT JUDGE YOU

I will not judge you, what you do
You must judge your act and deed
I have my own integrity
That I must guard for all my seed

Since we are equal in God's eye
To judge would put myself higher
Than where I belong by His law
And risk escaping the fire

INTO HEAVEN

Through the curtain into Heaven
I'd like the going a surprise
Maybe an hour would be all right
If reluctance did not arise

A ring for all to the Rapture
To rise together would be nice
But as long as it is Heaven
Then through death's door I think suffice

GRACE

A drunk moved slowly through the days
He staggered docks and wound his ways
For years he sailed the seven seas
And then he begged along the quays

The years went by, he like a bum
Craving liquor, rye, wine, and rum
Then one night when fog drifted low
Down from the dives he saw a glow

Something drew him from his plight
Through the fog like a moth to light
Out of the glow he heard singing
To his ears it drifted ringing

He walked into the open door
To the altar and knelt to floor
God gathered round and gave him life
Erased his days of drunken strife

It was the song *Amazing Grace*
That drew him there with its embrace
For he was dead but now will live
No greater gift that God can give

LIFE'S WALK

I have seen Satan in the night
Have seen him work in daytime light
Felt his tremors across the ground
Heard his scream in a distant sound

I have seen his death in season
Kill when he could for no reason
Have seen him rise in someone's son
Someone's daughter put on the run

I have walked beneath skies of gray
Not sure about the right of way
Walked on the banks of winding streams
And compromised with goals and dreams

I have seen sunshine golden bright
Had my heart yearn again for light
Found peace in the shade of God's glow
And I know how it feels to know